CHANI
COMMUNICATIONS
FROM THE DEVIC
KINGDOM

Book One

BERYL CHARNLEY

Original transcription of the channelled work in the 1980's and 1990's by Beryl Charnley
Transcribed and typed by Gordon Charnley
Digital A5 formatted in 2010
2nd edition in 2017 by Heather Charnley

ISBN 978-1-907042-31-7

PURPLE SPIRIT PRESS
Heather Charnley,
2 Whitesmiths Cottages, Dalston,
Carlisle, Cumbria, CA5 7QF.
Tel: (01228) 711050
Email: purplespiritpress@hotmail.co.uk
www.heathersvisionarygallery.co.uk

There are many more channelled works being issued all the time, as well as other topics.

Please contact if you wish to have more details.

CHANNELLED COMMUNICATIONS FROM THE DEVIC KINGDOM
Book One

CONTENTS

Channelled by Beryl Charnley

Channelled Communications from the Devic Kingdom
Foreword by Beryl Charnley

Teachings by Archangel Uriel, Achillion and others

Notes about the Channelled Teachings:

The devas or landscape angels began communicating with me once I began to have the confidence of knowing this was possible. It was somewhat of a surprise initially, and quite unexpected, but nevertheless wonderful.

The devas undertake to care for and nurture their own domain, which extends over quite a large area of countryside. Each deva has his or her own area to oversee, and whenever anyone can hear their thoughts, they are really delighted and greet you warmly wherever you arrive there. Normally it has been woodland areas that I connect with them, even in different countries we have visited on holiday, which is interesting despite the difference in language! Fortunately, in universal realms there is no language barrier through thought and knows no bounds.

I have also received messages from the 'little people' who normally communicate when I am close to a stream or river, and are full of fun.

I have a photograph that was taken in local woodland, and in the foreground stands a dear little fairy called Olivia, and in the background is a large bright being called Achillion who overlights the wood, and he was the first deva who communicated with me, and this is the only image I have of such beings and is therefore most precious!

Beryl Charnley

FOREWORD BY ACHILLION

DEVAS AND THEIR PLACE
IN THE ANGELIC HIERARCHY

We, the Devas or Landscape Angels, as we are known, overlight the areas of our particular part of the Earth, and we are closely connected with nature as a result, and also with mankind. We are virtually on a par with your guides, although we have not incarnated, and therefore we are in the lower section, shall we say, of the Angelic Beings, below the Archangels.

We are called Shining Ones in certain parts of the world, but then all Angels are, because from your point of view we are shining energies of light, and if you were to try to depict us as an artist would, then we would be shown as Shining Lighted Beings, and we are quite large in comparison with humans. Our size is variable, but generally it might be described as being about ten to twelve feet from head to toe, and we have plumes of light that make us appear as though we have wings!

The Archangels of course are larger Beings of great brilliance, and if you compare them with yourselves there is just not any way to describe them apart from being large brilliant Beings, larger than ourselves, but of such wonderful colours and beauteous appearance that the human eye cannot imagine.

Colours on the higher realms cannot compare with those upon Earth, however beautiful. There are many more varied and subtle colourings where we exist.

COMMUNICATIONS FROM THE DEVIC KINGDOM 1
ARCHANGEL URIEL-1

Greetings to you, this is Uriel. We have linked our minds together before and I am happy to speak to you and through you. My task is dealing with all of nature and together with the devas who work with me, I control the growth and beauty around you. You are aware of this beauty and as you have become more sensitive over the years, and the beauty seems to increase as years progress. It is because you are truly more aware of it, and see it with clearer eyes.

Some who work with me have spoken with you before, and I am aware of this, and I know that you delight in hearing from these Landscape Angels or Devas, and have done so over the past few years, both in this country and in other countries where you have travelled, some of whom are extremely wise and experienced. By experienced I mean that they have dwelt in that area for aeons, and this, as you are aware, shows that they have learnt much in their work. Some of them spoke to you in Cyprus, and had resided in the ocean bed before the island that exists now had risen due to volcanic activity. They were mountain devas and are vast beings of light, not as large as the Archangels, but extremely large compared with the normal Landscape Devas who are usually between twenty and thirty feet high. This is an approximate height, and the devas who spoke from the Cyprus mountains in the Troodos area were ten times that size, and although you could not see them, you were aware of great power around you.

It would be wonderful for you to be able to see both the devas and ourselves, and many other beings of light, and this will occur in future times. Some of mankind are conscious of and can see beings of light through their minds, the third eye area, and these indeed are blessed because they are few and far between. Most of humanity are completely unaware of us, and live their lives without the knowledge of the devic kingdom, which is rather sad but obviously this is a nebulous area, and we the archangels are aware of this. The only reference to the archangels is usually only in the Bible and this may not be read very often in a lifetime. So, unless those of whom I speak go to church on a regular basis, perhaps they do not even know of Raphael or myself. Perhaps we are lesser known to you, the two main archangels being Michael and Gabriel, and they too have spoken through this channel, and are known to all of you who read these words. But perhaps Uriel, Raphael, and myself you are not so aware of; we work in conjunction with all the Angelic Hierarchy and the Masters. We all serve God, and we all do our utmost to help the Earth in various ways, Raphael in his healing work with the healing angels, and I with the devic kingdom.

Naturally, in my work I appreciate any help given to me from yourselves, and therefore I was delighted that we were included in your meditation night, quite recently. As you know, time does not exist for us, but hopefully in the future we will be referred to again in your meditative work, and I will join with you at such times. We have been watching over you, the Golden Group, but to be included and mentioned in this gives us great pleasure. So be assured that whenever we are included in anything, we rush forward with eagerness, and will help in any way we can in future days with the work that you are doing.

In time to come I hope you will become more aware of me. I am a very great being of light, and I have mentioned the size of the Landscape Angels previously, and those in Cyprus being about a hundred feet in height, roughly, perhaps a little more. The Archangels are vast and are larger than any of the Landscape Devas, and my colours, if you are interested, are all the colours of nature, brilliant greens, golds and tinges of warm russet brown, and several flame colours, you cannot imagine how I might look to those who can see me clairvoyantly, but perhaps in time to come. Gabriel and Michael have been seen by some, but Raphael and myself are usually in the background. We are used to this and we do not mind because we do what we can in service to the Earth and God.

We are always happy in our work and in our linking together, we use the power of light as you have learnt to do, and our light is shone upon the Earth and all that grows. I am speaking now of myself and the landscape devas, also the smaller individual devas work in conjunction with myself as the head of things, like a general in command of his troops. The small devas work individually, and there are tree devas who are perhaps the largest of the individual smaller ones, and they are sometimes very old too and quite experienced, especially when you find an ancient oak tree, or a great redwood in the United States. All of these ancient trees have devas within them that have seen many things in their time, and if you could speak to them, which some of you have, you would find that they are very knowledgeable, and that they can tell you many truths about humanity.

The smaller devas individual to groups of plants and flowers are very fast in their vibratory rate compared with humanity, as we all are of course, but they, like the little people who are also part of the devic kingdom, are very light and small compared with ourselves. Perhaps light is not the word, but they move faster in their work, and can perhaps be likened to butterflies flitting around. They are beautiful little beings, and I know that you would love to be able to see all these very small beings of light, and in time to come you will. This will enrich your lives, and you will find great delight in watching them at their work and play, because they are allowed some leisure time like yourselves. Life would not be worth living if you did not have some time for pleasure.

Life is what you make it. There are some who do not know how to enjoy their lives, which is sad. Some of the humans that we watch do not know how to relax. They work and work, and feel that this is what they must do all their lives, and perhaps do not realise that there are many sides to a human's life. There is, of course, the physical working side and the leisure part of life, in which you can enjoy many hours of pleasure in different ways, whatever suits you. Either playing some game or relaxing on a beach, or in the countryside, or climbing mountains, which many find a challenge to them and worthwhile. There are so many sides to man's nature, and therefore he can go through his life in this way without using his spirituality, which as you have discovered is most important, and links you with many realms of which you might have been unaware of otherwise.

Once you have awakened to that inner life, it can never be lost to you, so it is comforting to know that you can link at any time you wish to be still, in order to hear that inner voice speaking to you. When you link with us, we come into your auric space and we realise that some of you are not aware of this. We are then a part of your consciousness, your super consciousness shall we call it, the part that is not within your body but a part of the whole unconscious mind. You realise that the physical side of you represents you while you are incarnating, but there is a greater part of you, which is not enclosed in a physical body. Part of it is, but mostly it is free to link with other beings of light. So long as you say a prayer or invocation before you begin, you are protected, and of course as you know, when you finish linking with us you should always close your chakras down. To us they look like beautiful coloured flowers that are all around you, they are not just in one spot as you might imagine, but glow beautifully with a metallic hue, and you are gradually growing extra chakras above you that are becoming more obvious and beautiful to us in the realms of light.

As you bring down light from the Christ Star or from the Source, whatever you wish to call the Godhead, you unite with that as it comes through you and down into the Earth. Your light rises up to meet the light from above, so that you become one as you meditate, and use that light for good. We are delighted that so many have become lightworkers over the past few years and are radiating that light to many places that really need that help and support. The Earth herself needs light because there has been much pollution over the many years, and much pollutants have filled the seas and waterways, and we have been helping to counteract this in whatever way we can, but sadly there has been a loss of life because of man's pollution, and we hope that now he is realising what has happened and will do more to counteract this. We have been attempting to communicate with many over the years, and we feel that perhaps now the turning point has been reached, and there is a change in man's thinking. Even the air has been affected, as you know, and the ozone layer that was drastically affected, is gradually closing up and improving as man has altered his ways.

I hope to speak to you all again, but in the meantime I am sure that my devas will contribute to the book that I hope will come to pass in the future. In the meantime, God bless and keep you all. **Uriel.**

COMMUNICATIONS FROM THE DEVIC KINGDOM 1
ARCHANGEL URIEL-2

My greetings to you, this is Uriel. This is a beautiful special still day in September with everything glinting in the sunshine; it is a day of great beauty and fruitfulness. This time of year has been spoken of through poets in majestic terms, so I will not try to better them! Suffice to say that I hope that all of mankind appreciates the beauty of this day. I know that in other parts of the world it will be completely different, and is, but here at the present it is still and shining. The small devas have been busy as they always are, and have been helping fruits and berries to form, which you see around you. Each time of the year has something special to give, and this is the season of fruitfulness and expansion. The leaves of the trees are full and have not as yet begun to fall and become dry and withered. It is a beautiful time of year here in England, and although it is green and pleasant, it is still filled with violent thoughts from those who do not appreciate the beauty.

There is always an element of violence with mankind, and we hope that in time to come all men will be freed from that evil that has been prevalent over the centuries. It is just a small percentage of mankind that has this within them, and in time perhaps, love will overcome the dark negative nature of these people. It has been noticed that recently the crime level has been high due to drug intake. This is a very serious element in society, and I know that it is something that is being gradually eliminated, but there is a worldwide group spreading these drugs and affecting many young people, and sadly so many have lost their lives either completely or virtually, because they have affected their souls through this. Those people who traffic in drugs have a lot to answer for, and will have a large amount of karma to repay. The fact is that they will have other lifetimes to lead in order to repay this on another third dimensional planet.

There are many of you now who have reached the point of no return, which means that you will not need to reincarnate again. Those of you who read these words have discovered that due to your spiritual awakening, you will be able to raise yourselves and ascend onto the fourth and then the fifth dimension. You have gained knowledge of the ancient wisdom sufficiently and your spirituality has lifted you onto a higher level of thinking. This is a wonderful thing, and there are now sufficient numbers of you to warrant the Earth rising upwards with the majority of mankind onto that higher level of being. So there is much for you to look forward to in this respect, because you will be able to see so many things that at present you are completely unaware of. The Archangels have been helping increasingly over these last few decades, associating with humanity to try to communicate with many of you, and gradually you are able to reach up to our level of being. This is wonderful for us to be able to contact humanity, and I have spoken to many people across the world now, on occasions. Those who have been in contact with Michael and Gabriel are now increasing their ability, to hear from myself and of course many other beings of light.

We ourselves have been uplifting the consciousness of the devic kingdom, and they too are progressing. I know that it had not occurred to you that the devas would be evolving the same as you are, but all of us are attempting to lift ourselves consciously throughout our existence, I will not say lifetime because we have a different stream of consciousness from humanity. We have not incarnated and therefore our existence is constant, unlike mankind, who keeps returning and evolving through different lifetimes. We exist constantly, but are still attempting to rise upwards higher and higher, and serve God in more exalted ways. As I work with the nature kingdom, I attempt to bring the devic kingdom constantly on to a higher level. The little people evolve slightly differently, but I am also in charge of them. It is a constant joy to me to be able to guide and raise them onto higher levels of being. I watch and help them in many ways. The devas of each plant, flower and tree give of their essence to those growing things, and I too in my work give of my very being to everything that is connected with the Earth and nature in all its glory, and it is a wonderful task that I have to protect and help the Earth in this way.

The Earth herself has been affected, as you know in many ways, through pollution and ravishment, because man in his thoughtlessness has done great damage over the last century. Pollution has been rampant, and hopefully mankind is seeing the error of his ways, and will right things, but it will take some time before this eventually will take effect. There are many things which have happened, sometimes by accident, but sometimes knowingly, and oceans have been affected greatly by oil and manufacturing products causing effluent. Over the last fifty years it has become apparent that man must mend his ways or else the Earth would have to retaliate in some way. Fortunately mankind has at last begun to repair some of the damage.

I am obviously not blaming you, and any who read these words, for you are all very aware of the ecology and attempt to protect it wherever you can. As you know, even the ozone layer surrounding the Earth had been affected in many ways, and is improving since it was discovered in dismay that aerosols and other items had affected it adversely, creating that hole, particularly over America.

Gradually this is closing up, and you will find that there will be less danger of skin cancer, but always be protected, as it is dangerous to remain in brilliant sunshine for a long time without protecting the skin. Most people are conscious of this now, and take precautions using creams to protect their children especially.

This is a wonderful time of awakening for mankind, and you and others have been expanding your minds, thoughts and consciousness, and over these last few years increasingly more of humanity has become uplifted. It is with great pleasure that we see this, and know that the energies that we have been pouring down upon Earth are gradually taking effect, and this capability of expanding the consciousness has been accelerating over time. All of you are speeding up this process wherever possible in daily meditations, in reaching out towards those on the higher realms.

I, Uriel, am delighted that so many are now aware of the devic kingdom and the Angelic Hierarchy. We have been working in conjunction with the Masters and the beings from space over a number of years. Those from the stars that you are aware of, the Pleiades, Arcturus and particularly Sirius have been joining with us for so long, and from other star systems of which you know a little, from Alpha Centauri and Andromeda, and others such as Betelgeuse and Lyra have been communicating with some of you who have been attempting to raise their consciousness towards them. It is wonderful that this is so because we have all been attempting to send our thoughts and energies towards you all for such a long time, that at last these efforts are now bearing fruit, and communications have been made with quite a number upon the Earth now.

I hope that there will be many communications made between the devic kingdom and this channel in order to compose this book about the devic kingdom, and man's working together with the devas to make the Earth a more beautiful and wonderful place in which to live. There are many Landscape Angels as you might call them, the large devas who control the smaller devas in their areas throughout the world. They cover many miles of territory, and are truly proud of the work that they do, and they work with me very closely in protecting the guiding the devic work on the Earth. I hope that you will enjoy reading the words, which are written by these beings of light, and I know that they will be working towards the benefit of their areas throughout the Earth in communicating with you. I look forward to speaking to you again in the future, but in the meantime, I give you my blessing this day, Uriel.

11

COMMUNICATIONS FROM THE DEVIC KINGDOM 1
ACHILLION THE DEVA-3

My greetings to you, this is Achillion. I am very happy to be the first deva to start on this book about the Devic Kingdom and its relationship to humanity. It is a very vast subject, so I will just say what I feel is most important, and make suggestions for the inter-relationship of our world and your own. We are two sides of the coin, shall we say. We are on the spiritual side, and you are on the physical side, although you have within you your own spirituality and that is what I am appealing to now. Your own spirituality makes you aware of beings of light and the linking between the world of the spirit and the physical world. Some of you are capable of linking between the two realms and this is fortunate, because as a result we can speak through these channels in order to make our thoughts known to you. Some of you are in touch with your guides and this is good as it helps you through your lifetime to keep on the straight and narrow, shall we say.

Mankind over the last century has in general been polluting the atmosphere and the Earth herself, and of late it has become extremely severe in certain areas, although fortunately there have been programmes on television that have made the younger generation in particular much more aware of what man is doing to the planet herself. As a result, the young people are attempting to create a better balance between humanity and nature. There has been suffering in the past decades, which has been extremely sad because the pollution of the oceans has caused devastation to the population of those areas. Everything that lives within that watery depth has been affected in some way, and although there is still a culling of seals, I believe that gradually this will be reduced because the numbers have been naturally reducing as a result of the pollution, and it will be unnecessary for man to play this part.

We often do not understand the minds of men, we do not speak of you, but those who have caused great suffering to both these marine creatures and all the beasts that live upon the Earth that are used for domestic purposes. By that I mean particularly what had happened to beef cattle that had been subjected to the mad cow disease, purely through foodstuffs totally unsuitable for herbivorous creatures. The resultant slaughter was unimaginable in numbers, and extremely sad for all concerned, both to the farmers who were affected, and to ourselves who were directly linked with nature in any way. We know you too were saddened that so many creatures had to be killed as a result of the stupidity of some manufacturers who had included the remains of other animals in the cattle food, thereby making the cattle cannibals.

I am sure that in time many more of humanity will stop eating meat and any living creatures, and will find that their diet will consist of vegetables, pulses and nuts, anything that is grown from the Earth rather than creatures that live upon it. People are becoming more perceptive in

12

their thoughts about diet, and recognise the fact that they do not need to kill to eat, and that life can carry on without the killing of creatures that have as much right to live as you yourselves. I think that most who read these words will have that thought in mind in any case, and most of you do not eat living beings. It is something that has gradually become more acceptable, and people are much more aware of the food that has been prepared for them, or which they themselves prepare, and that it is far better just to eat natural products instead of something that has been living, that like yourselves is flesh and blood.

As time progresses, mankind is thinking more of the Earth as a living being, a sentient being that has it's life blood, the rivers and streams, and has as its flesh, the fertile valleys and mountains, and all that clothe it, such as trees and all vegetation, whether flowering or not, and this is the part of creation that we take care of. It is the Devic Kingdom, the devas, the Landscape Angels, who are in charge of this part of the Earth, and the growing things, and we take great pleasure in producing beautiful areas throughout the world. Each landscape angel or deva has his own territory, I say his because most of the devas are of the masculine gender, but there are always exceptions to the rule.

We cover quite vast acreages of land, and this channel is aware I in particular cover the area from Slaley across a wide band of the countryside to Hexham, right up to the river's edge. This covers quite a number of miles to either side, so it is quite a large area, and each deva, like myself, has a similar area of the Earth that is their own territory, and under whom the small individual devas and little people do their work. They cause their essence to be put into the trees, shrubs, flowers and all growing things, and each individual deva is in my charge.

There is much pleasure involved in producing beauty in this way. Throughout the cycle of seasons, the devas have work to do and they do it willingly and happily, knowing that their life's work is to serve, and this is something that the angelic kingdom live to do. The devic kingdom is a branch of the Angelic Hierarchy, and that is our life, to serve God, and to serve all. We know that your lives are different, for you have your own free will, the choice to do whatever you wish to do, but I think that most who read these words have a dedication to serve in some way. To either serve mankind, or to serve mankind and God, and we feel that you are on the spiritual path towards upliftment to that higher dimension that you wish to attain. It is hoped that all of humanity will in time reach this level of thinking, and put aside all violent, evil thoughts and deeds, and become one with those who have more love in their hearts, and who have that light within them, which you have.

There is also that spiritual light that you have been working with for some years which has been brought down from the realms of light, I am aware that you are all light workers and as such you are attempting to do more with your lives than just live the normal physical existence which many do and have no idea that there can be any other life. I know that you

13

have friends who are good people, perhaps but who cannot accept this new spirituality which you all are work for. They perhaps think that it is strange to concentrate on meditation for part of your daily discipline, and perhaps they will never try to link with their guide or others in the higher realms, but this does not matter if they are genuinely good people. It is those who are of a more violent disposition that we are hoping will raise themselves out of the mire and join those standing in the light to provide a better world for all.

Perhaps some of you are able to see us, I believe you can, but most of you until you reach that higher dimension are only aware of our existence through those who can either see or hear us, and perhaps you are wondering what our appearance is? We are pure fountains of light and of many colours; usually our size is roughly about twenty to thirty feet high. This is the landscape angel I am speaking of, myself included. I, myself have colours that are of blue, turquoise and silver, mostly those pastel shades, whereas others may be completely different in hue. But it is difficult perhaps to describe ourselves because we are rather nebulous in shape, so it would be difficult for anyone to paint us I would think! I think that the fountain of light is a fairly good description.

The individual devas for each plant and flower are considerably smaller than ourselves, and they again are light beings which are of various sizes, mostly no higher than a foot, and vary again in colour and substance. Perhaps you might catch a glimpse of something out of the corner of your eye like a butterfly speeding past, although they do not fly very fast do they, but that perhaps might have been a small deva showing itself to you. They are very timid and shy, and as they are on another dimension, they cannot normally be seen by humanity.

On the higher dimensions our vibratory rate is much faster than that of the third dimension, and therefore it is normally impossible for the human eye to see us, however, in time you will and we look forward to meeting you face to face one day. In the meantime, I give you my blessing this day and hope that I may speak once again towards the end of this book. God bless.
Achillion.

14

COMMUNICATIONS FROM THE DEVIC KINGDOM 1
THE DEVAS OF TROODOS-4

We are very happy to greet you once more. It is some time since we spoke to you, and we are very honoured because we realise that this communication is for this book compiled with information from other landscape angels or devas, and we are very happy to be included in this book and to take part in it. We will explain who we are. We are the devas of a mountainous region in Cyprus called the Troodos, and this particular point is where we have spoken to you previously. It is a place of great beauty and peace in the island, with tree covered hills and the mountains beyond. We, the devas of this area speak as one voice. As we have said previously to you, the channel, we are great beings of light, ten times larger than the normal landscape angels or devas who have their own territories across the world. All vary in size, but we are very old large beings of light who dwelt once upon the ocean bed, and as the island of Cyprus rose from that ocean bed, so we ourselves did, and we have existed since those days.

Therefore, we have experienced much time, and much in the way of happenings on this island. There have been various civilisations living upon it, and at present it is those who are of the Greek Orthodox Church in the main, but as you are aware, there are many nationalities who visit the island throughout the year, because it is a pleasant climate here, it draws people from near and far. Once people have visited this island, they return many times as a rule if they feel drawn to it, as you do, because of the nature of the place. Here in the mountainous region there is inspiration for all if they will tune in to what is here, the nature kingdom and this mountainous region, which is full of spirituality. As you and others have seen, there are monasteries that are scattered throughout this hilltop area of the island. There are many monasteries, and the main one nearby, the Kyykos is the one that draws most people. It has a beautiful air of peace, and this is understandable because of the many prayers that have been said over the years it has existed.

We feel that it is rather sad that the island is divided, and it is mainly because of power. Those who seek power are always the ones who are at fault. This whole island should belong to the Greek Cypriots, and we know in time that it will be so once more, but in the meantime there is always some turmoil between the two races. The Cypriots and the Turkish who have invaded the land, and have been here for several decades now, in that northern part of the island where the division is, and we are sad that this is so. Man, always greedy for power, it is the way of humanity unfortunately. We are aware that not all of you have this need for power, but there is always an element that is never happy until they have gained power over others, and are supreme to their way of thinking, perhaps, but not really in the eyes of God. All men are equal in His eyes,

15

and we ourselves have seen many come and go on this island of beauty and spirituality.

It is not often that we have the opportunity to speak our thoughts to those like yourselves who are keen to evolve their spirituality in their physical life. There are those who live good lives and attend church as many do, but they do not wish to expand their consciousness as you are doing, those who read these words. Perhaps they are unaware that this is possible, and we are sure that in time, many more of mankind will learn to do this. It takes time for you to realise the potential that man has in exploring his capabilities in this direction, and we know that those of you reading this have been attempting to reach up to higher levels of consciousness for some time, and we are glad that this is so, and that you are turning towards the realms of light, those realms in which we live and many have their being. There are some who are able to see both ourselves and many other beings of light. They are indeed fortunate, and gradually I am sure that all of you will be able to expand your consciousness even further in order to do this; then it will be wonderful for you to both see and hear us, because in time all of you who are working towards this upliftment of your consciousness on to a higher vibration will be able to hear and see us.

All of you have different abilities, there are some like the channel who can hear our thoughts and know that they are from us or other beings. It is perhaps a nebulous way of communication, but those who genuinely channel from the realms of light to yourselves are capable of differentiating between the different beings, although unseen, it is quite clear as to who it is thinking towards you. It is telepathy in a way although not telepathy between those on the physical world, but linking between the two worlds rather like a radio station. That is how we communicate with humanity through channels such as this one, who is sending forth our thoughts towards you in a clear manner. Those of us who live in the realms of light are dependent on such as she to give our thoughts to all who are interested in this work. We hope that we will be able to communicate further at another time because there is so much to say.

We are conscious of the fact that there is much of humanity that is at war, who are constantly causing others to suffer through this. There are outbreaks of fighting in many places across the world, and as a result, there are many losing their lives, maimed or starved as a result. We hope that these warring factions will eventually become peaceful and attempt to live life as it is hoped mankind will in the future, in peace with one another without wishing to wrest power from those who need the land for themselves. We hope that in time they will see the error of their ways and come to realise that it is totally unnecessary. There is nothing to be gained from fighting and certainly nothing to be gained spiritually because through killing others, it causes a problem within the soul of those who kill. It is something that can never be recovered from in a lifetime. As you know, karma works for and against you. If you live a good life, then you will receive all the benefits in the next life. It will be as though you had been reborn to receive the benefits that you deserve as a result of that good life, but if you have committed many crimes, killed people or been evil in your lifetime, then in the next life you would have received much bad karma and you would have to repay this by being disabled, blinded, or disadvantaged in some way.

But now has come the time when there will be no more karma, so that those who have committed evil in this lifetime will be swept aside. As you have been told, this is your last lifetime upon the world because you are all at the point when you will be moving upwards with the Earth on to that fourth dimension, and subsequently the fifth, which is what you are working towards now. Those who have committed evil as we have said, will be swept aside, and when the time comes for them to reincarnate, it will be on another third dimensional world or star, of which there are not many, because each star and planet has been moving upwards onto higher dimensions as time has progressed. But those of you who have been living good lives will not return; this is your last lifetime of really physical existence. In the future it will be on a finer vibratory level that you will live, so that your bodies will become less solid, and more amorphous, and you will not need much in the way of solid food. Everything is changing, and gradually the Earth herself is changing also.

There is nothing obvious about it, it is just a gradual process, because if you look around you, everything seems solid to you, and the trees, mountains, rivers and streams, still appears to be the same, and yet gradually the molecular structure of everything is altering, subtly and imperceptibly changing, so that it will never be as solid as it was when first you were born. Things have been altering over the last decades, and you would find, if you were able to see clairvoyantly, that the structure of everything has altered, so that it is becoming more like it is upon the higher realms, and gradually you will be able to see this happening. You are improving gradually, slowly but surely, to learn to hear clairaudiently, telepathically, until more beings will be able to speak to you and through you as this channel is doing, so that in a short space of time, all of you on the spiritual path will be capable of receiving communications between the two worlds, the world of light and the Earth. You are all becoming capable of hearing from us, and we look forward to the time when we can communicate with all of you in time.

All you need now is faith, and to believe in what we say, which is the truth. Sometimes it is difficult to believe that all these things are occurring, but the truth is there for all to see, and in time to come, it will be proved that these communications from ourselves and so many others are the truth, and we are sure that in time all will accept it. We give you our blessing this day and hope to speak once more. God bless and keep you all.

The Devas of Troodos

COMMUNICATIONS FROM THE DEVIC KINGDOM 1
ARCHANGEL MICHAEL-5 (from Cyprus)

Yes it is I, Michael, who greets you this day. I am pleased to offer you my contribution to your book. This island of Cyprus is full of contrasts, the beautiful coastline and resorts filled with people in the sunshine, that is the material side of the island, shall we say, and the bustling nightlife that appeals to some. Yet the central part of the island that is very arid, with little vegetation in places that seems to be so sparse, and yet it is filled with spirituality and peace. It is where many visions have been seen in the past, particularly in the mountainous regions of the Troodos area. Naturally where the monasteries have been sited, they have been there for many centuries, as a result there is great spirituality exuding from these buildings and from those who live there.

We have been watching humanity on this island for centuries, and we understand how tourism has altered it greatly. As the years have gone by, many resorts have been built, and wealth has come to the island as a result. This has happened throughout the world because people are able to travel more freely now, but it is important to keep that sense of spirituality, and this is what we hope will still remain on the island, and the negativity of these coastal areas where nightlife abounds must be counteracted by light. So, it is important that mankind will keep this in mind, and work with us and all the devic kingdoms who exist upon the island and throughout the whole world.

The devic kingdom is divided into levels. The Archangels are the highest level of the devic kingdom, and naturally the angelic realms are quite complex, but I speak today about the landscape angels and those who serve them. You have already been contacted by the landscape angels, the devas of this area in the Troodos region, and I am sure that they are pleased to be able to communicate with anyone on the physical plane. They are very large beings of light, which I am sure they will explain, is a result of them living in the mountainous region, and they are in charge of all smaller devas. Each landscape angel dominates a territory throughout the Earth, and these can be quite extensive in some places. In Cyprus there are a number of devas, landscape angels who may communicate with you in the future, but it is to the Troodos region that you, the channel, usually come for inspiration.

There are smaller devas who work with the landscape angels. The tree devas, many of whom are quite ancient beings who exist within the trees. Each tree has within it a large or small deva, depending on the age of the tree, and those who have been here for many years are quite wise, and it is possible to tune in to these devas, as it is possible to tune in to any beings of light like ourselves. Besides the tree devas there are individual devas for each growing things, be it a plant of some kind or vegetables or flowers, everything has within it a glowing being, and it is to these that the little people attune and bring their essence. It is important that all humanity becomes aware of these beings of light, some of which are extremely minute and yet all have their purpose for being. It is a completely different stream of consciousness from that of humanity, and it is important that all of you are aware that mankind is needed to help the devic kingdom at this time. He is a caretaker of the Earth after all, Mother Earth, and we hope that there will be even more linking together between mankind and the devic kingdom in the future. We know that more people are becoming aware that the Earth is a living entity, and that it is important that pollution lowers its levels. The young people of today are much more aware of this than in the past, and many programmes on television have been devoted to this subject, which is very rewarding for us to see, so that the word is put out to all, that protection must be given to the Earth and all that lives upon it, all growing things, animals and humanity alike.

I was very honoured at the time when the invocation was brought through from Master R, which summons me forth to help mankind at this time of change. It was brought through by this channel, and although quite short is an important invocation that I shall now repeat:

'Wielder of the sword of light come forth
Defend man from his darkness
May God's pure divine light shine through the hearts of men
And love and peace prevail.'

Try to use this invocation daily, as it has power because it involves myself, Michael, to bring light to mankind and to spread the light throughout the Earth. All of you who read these words are light workers, and have been so for a number of years. It is good that this is so, and we know that you have the Earth at heart, and all who live upon it. The light is becoming more powerful now, as a result of our sending energies towards the Earth over the past decades, and we have been watching the accumulation of these energies becoming more powerful within you and others of like mind. The Earth too has benefited, and as a result, has been able to withstand much of the pollution. We are glad that all are relating to these energies, and you are gradually becoming aware of them yourselves.

Everything is changing at this time, and I am sure that although it is subtle, you are finding that more people are able to be sensitive to the changes around them. It is an enlightening time for all, and those who are sensitive are becoming more able to reach their consciousness on to a higher level, so that beings of light can channel communications to them in different ways. Not everyone is able to hear thoughts in their minds, but this does not matter, for many people see symbols of some kind given to them in meditation. It matters not what you receive, but as long as you a dedicated in linking with the world of light, you will gradually become to hear our thoughts quite clearly, and as you raise higher wi consciousness, this will enable you to link with us much mor rather like man when he first came upon the Earth and was touch with God. You too will become changed in this way, and I am sure that all of you will be happy for this to occur.

You have been told about the photon belt that has been coming closer to the Earth, and as it is in a high dimension, scientists cannot forecast it. There is no instrument that can record something of this kind approaching. There are many scientific and electronic instruments that can record the stars, satellites, space vehicles, and many things that are near the Earth, but none can record something in a higher dimension. As the photon belt nears the Earth, you will be given plenty of warnings. It is slowly, inexorably coming closer, but it is difficult for any on any dimension whatsoever to say exactly when it will pass over the Earth. Everything will be cleansed in the process, including the Earth herself. It is difficult to say when this will happen for time is man made and is like an endless belt, that can run back or forwards. We can look into the future; the past and we can exist in the now. You can look back on the past but you cannot look too much into the future. It is better for you to live in the now on the physical world, but we find it hard to gauge when something of this kind will happen on the Earth. Suffice to say, inevitably it will pass over the Earth and change everything forever. There will be no more karmic lives, and no more reincarnations. Your life will continue in a slightly changed way, but you will not have to return to the Earth again to either pay or be repaid karma for that cycle of events will be over.

Many of us are working together for the good of humanity. As you know, there are other beings from stars that you were not aware of, but some have been contacting you and others over the last few years. Many beings have been working with us and with the Masters to help mankind to negotiate this change as easily as possible. Some changes are gradual and have been happening over recent decades, making people gradually more positive in outlook. You will be capable of doing many things you would never have dreamt of before. Use your abilities now to the full, those that you have developed, and extend this capability, particularly telepathy, because once the changes have occurred, you will need to be proficient in this as communications will be altered.

Just remember to have faith in us. You know that we are always protecting you and will safeguard all of you now and in the future. Work with the devic kingdom and they will reward you in many ways. They are happy to work with mankind, and have been devoted to working in service to God and the Earth, and have always wished that mankind would mend his ways in general. We are not speaking particularly of you, but man in general who is not aware of the devic kingdom. In the future I am sure there will be many changes in men's minds, and that your minds will become all powerful. It is a powerful tool used positively for the good of all. We know that you are capable of this in healing and sending light to the Earth, and to others who are in need of it, both on the Earth and in the cosmos. Have faith, and all will be well now and in the future. God bless you all. Michael.

20

COMMUNICATIONS FROM THE DEVIC KINGDOM 1
THE DEVAS OF TROODOS-6

We greet you today, our small friend, in the Troodos area once more.

We are very happy to say more on the subject of the devic kingdom. You have recognised our power and magnitude, and are aware of our presence here; it is necessary for you to have peace and quiet in order to concentrate on our words. Always we wish to tell mankind more about our work. Those of us who live in mountainous regions, as we have said previously, are very much larger devas than the majority who live on the plains. It is because it is necessary to have great strength in order to survive in this area. We live within the mountain, and as a result, power builds up from beneath the surface at sea level, shall we say, and therefore our power is much more than it would be had we lived on the plains. It is necessary, we find it difficult to explain, but it is so. Always we wish to try to explain what may seem strange to you, but is natural to the devic kingdom.

There are other devas who dwell on the sea level and lower areas of this island, and yet we do not have a great deal to do with them because they deal with different types of work from ourselves. We are in contact with other devas from mountains on the mainland and other parts of the world. It is because of this that we do not have so many dealings with those on our island, although naturally there is a linkup from time to time. The mountainous areas of the world have devas who link together in thought, word and deed, and we are a separate section of the devic kingdom as a result, nevertheless, all devas work together in conjunction to serve God and the Earth, to protect the Earth from many dangers that threaten it. We do what we can to conserve the ecology of the Earth, and we are very pleased to see that mankind is becoming increasingly much more aware and is being made aware of the pollution that is threatening the Earth at this time. More of the young people are learning about the environment and are concerned about it so it is good that this will continue. As they grow older, they will learn to cope with the vicissitudes of the Earth, and try to correct situations that have been the cause of great damage over recent decades.

It is time that the Earth was protected more by mankind. The devas can do so much, but they cannot control man and would not wish to try, therefore it is important to spread our word to as many as possible, so that mankind will continue to do more for the environment. Always we protect our own areas, and in this mountainous area of the Troodos region in Cyprus, it is necessary to protect the trees and wildlife. There are many species of animals that live on this island, and some of which are not seen anywhere else. I believe you have heard of the moufflon sheep that live in the forested area nearby, not in the present forest that you are in, but in the cedar wood area. This is a protected species fortunately, so we are

21

grateful for this, that it has been seen to be a tragedy to kill off these creatures that are unknown elsewhere. This is being done in other areas throughout the world. Certain species that live in only one area must be protected at all costs; otherwise they would die out completely, which would be extremely sad and unnecessary. If they are doing damage of course, then nature should be protected, and the appropriate trees, areas of grass or shrubs that is being eaten by those animals can be fenced off in some way.

However, we are concerned about the actual environment more than the animals in reality. Mankind has been gradually becoming aware of what has been done to the Earth in recent times, and we know that this place in particular is quite safe because it is looked upon as a special area of great natural interest. What is essential is that the whole of the environment of the world should be cared for and appreciated. So many places have become neglected, or the trees cut down, so that the protected area of the Earth where the trees grew is eroding away and becoming dry and desert-like in many places where forests were eradicated. What we hope for with man and what we feel is happening, is that large areas throughout the Earth are becoming protected, and being defended from those who would prey on it. Places that perhaps in the past have been open for all to visit are being fenced off, so that only those who will care for the area can enter.

It is sad for certain people who would wish to visit beauteous places and cannot now do so because of the misdemeanours of some, however if you look at it from our point of view, it is better this way, and these places can still be viewed from afar. Perhaps it is not the same as actually visiting the area, but on the other hand, if it is explained to people that it is for the protection of the ecology, we are sure that they will all understand. I know that there are places in your country of England that have had to be fenced off so that large numbers of people cannot visit these areas, and as a result, protection is being given to the vegetation. The surrounding area is recovering too from the many people who have walked upon it in the past, where damage has been done, causing erosion. Everything is understandable if it is explained, and it is most important that the whole of the Earth is cared for.

We are sure you are aware, that smaller devas protect individual specimens. There are devas that protect the trees, and in fact there is a deva inside each tree, which can become quite ancient in time. If the tree is extremely large and old, then that tree deva is very old and experienced. I think the one who channels these words has been aware of one or two of these quite elderly devas, and has attuned to them, which all of you can do and will do in time, we are sure. The time is coming when all will be able to attune to their guides, the devas, the little people and indeed to the Masters and many other beings that exist on higher dimensions, and who can also travel through time. We are able to travel through time ourselves,

22

we can travel into the future to discover what is ahead for ourselves and for mankind, and we have done so.

We think that you have been told before by other beings that there is much in store for you, good things that will improve your quality of life spiritually and things you could not even dream about. You have much to discover, but there is work to be done in order to reach these dizzy heights, and we know that those of you who are working on your spirituality, are gradually discovering what you are capable of, but you have only scratched the surface. You will be able to do things that at present only those on higher dimensions do, but you will work towards this and discover your many latent abilities. You are great beings of light compared with your small physical frames, and as you know, your auras extend far beyond you, depending how spiritually advanced you are.

We can see your lights coming towards us, and depending on your capabilities, the light shines very brightly from those of you who are spiritually aware and dwell on the path, but all of you are still learning, and there is much more ahead of you to cope with. We are delighted to speak to you at all and we have not communicated with many of mankind, and we are attempting to find what it is you are searching for. We know that all who read these words are attempting to increase their potential and capabilities, of raising the consciousness onto as high a level as possible. We do hope that many more of your civilisation will continue and attempt to do as you are doing, so that man will raise onto that higher level and become more as he was when man first came onto this Earth; more spiritual and in touch with God constantly. All of you are attempting this now, and we are aware that you wish to learn more each day.

Life is a journey of experience, it is like a river flowing towards the sea, and life means more to some than others. It is a great adventure, and this adventure brings you flowing towards that higher vibration, so that you rise upwards and join in that flow with others of like mind, and together you will journey towards the highest level you can. There will be no more separation, and there will be a unity that you have never known in your lives. When you reach that fifth dimension, you will join with throngs of other beings of light, and you will never know separation again. All are one, and all are working for the good of all. Once you have joined in that wonderful union, you will not wish to return to a third dimensional situation any more. Life will be a great joy, and you will be jubilant with that wonderful situation in which you will find yourselves in future days. We wish you well on your path to that great adventure, and we know that you all have a great goal ahead of you. That plan which is there for all, if they wish to seize the opportunity that is there for the asking; to evolve your souls onto as high a level as possible.

Now we wish to say farewell, but we hope that it is not forever. We hope that we will be able to join together in thought again in future days. God bless and keep you all.
The Devas of Troodos

COMMUNICATIONS FROM THE DEVIC KINGDOM 1
MARCOS THE DEVA-7 (at Treetops, Wark)

I am happy to greet you this day, this is Marcos and I am delighted that it is possible to speak even in the snow time, because few people are around to contact at this time of year. In fact, there are very few in any case who are able to be in touch with myself at any time of year. So I am very pleased to welcome you and the others who will read these words. You have compiled communications from several beings of light for this book, and I am very happy to be among that group of beings. All of us are enthusiastic about spreading our words to humanity. I know that all of you who read this are aware of the state of the planet at this time, and we are concerned about it, and are doing our utmost to right it, and to put aright the minds of men. Fortunately, there has been a change in the outlook of much of mankind over recent years, and gradually the young people are helping to spread the word that the planet must be taken care of. We have been instilling that into the minds of all with whom we come in contact.

The planet Earth, Gaia, the Mother, is the most important thing in your lives. You are all dependent upon the Earth for your very lives, and you know that the Earth herself has been going through a troubled time. There have been many ravages of the Earth over recent decades, and pollution has been at its highest level, but now things are gradually changing, fortunately, although there is still much to be done to put things right, and allow new growth. What is necessary is for all mankind to be able to take part, and participate in the work ahead. You are aware that changes have been happening over the last ten years, that the dimensions are changing and the Earth has been rising onto the fourth dimension, slowly but surely, and in time that will have been completed. You have been altering and are aware of change both within and around you. The minds of men have been awakened and there has been a great expansion of consciousness throughout the world for those who are awakened. Those souls who are participating in light work at this time, like you, have been attempting to spread the word to others who have perhaps not been aware of what is happening.

It is a time of great exhilaration for all of you because things will never return to what you might call 'normal' again. They will continue to improve, and the Earth herself will provide much in the way of sustenance for you. It may not be what you would normally call food, but the food that you will breathe in will be rather like the manna from heaven, which was mentioned in the Bible. It will be provided for all, and no one will go hungry in the future, the climate as you are aware, has been changing, and will be more equable for all in future times. You will find that these long winters will diminish eventually as the Earth moves into that higher dimension, and you will be ready to accept this I know. You will be only too pleased to accept this I think! However, to be more serious, all beings who live on this planet will be raised onto the fourth and then the fifth dimensions, and you and others will lead the way. Those who are already awakened will lead those who are following on, and you will be the vanguard. Some have already moved and ascended onto this higher level, but you will not be far behind.

In future days, you will experience more change in your levels of consciousness. You will find it easier to direct your consciousness onto that new level, and as a result you will help to bring about this ascension more swiftly than it might have been. You are all gradually becoming aware that the fourth dimension is close, and that it is all around you, and that you only have to step into it through your mind's power. I think that all of the devic kingdom are delighted with the progress that man is making in his life. I know that there is always the negative side, and that there are still men of violence abroad in parts of the world, but believe me, this will be overcome and light will prevail. We have long hoped for this change to come about, and we know that you have been doing your part in sending light to those dark places, to the negativity within the Earth and to those minds that are closed, and attempting to pull down those veils of ignorance and fear, and sending forth light and love to all. This is all part of God's plan for humanity and the Earth. We hope that we can play our part in this and guide you in whatever way you need help.

The devic kingdom is wide. There are many devas who have been contacting humanity over the past few years and this is proliferating. More people are attuning to the realms of light, and in time all will be able to contact us, and so many beings exist of which you are unaware. I know that you are aware of beings from other stars are amongst you on a different dimension, and from a different time occasionally, but they too are very pleased to be able to contact some of you, and in time all of you will be able to both see and hear these beings. They have been helping to acclimatise all of you to the idea that they are here to help and have been in existence here for many years. They have been encircling the Earth in their ships, and helping to adjust people's thoughts and outlook for the future. They too have gone through this transition stage from one dimension to another several times, and so they have that experience behind them. They work for the good of the whole, for God and the Angelic Hierarchy who are linking with them and the Masters always, and all these beings of light, and ones from other stars are here to guide you as we are.

Remember that your spirituality is that all-important part of you that has continued through lifetimes, and has brought you to this point. We are all beings of light, but you have the physical body to contend with on a material world, and at present it is difficult to see very far ahead of you. But all is very well, for you are treading the spiritual path, and you will move on to better things. You are aware of what is occurring and this is important, because once you are aware you will never look back and only forward into the light. As I said before, the devic kingdom is vast and includes many beings of light. Apart from the devas, the large landscape angels like myself, there are small devas, as has been said previously by another deva, individual devas for each part of the vegetable kingdom, although many of the tree devas are large. There are also the devas who live in the water, the undines, who have communicated to many over time and still will do so, also the sylphs of the air who are more difficult to contact, but are available for communication on occasions, and of course the little people of whom there are many. It is hoped that perhaps they may say a word or two today if we are fortunate, we will see.

'Yes we are here, and this is our domain, and we are very pleased to see you this day. It is fortunate that you were able to come despite the weather. We have often seen you in the garden and are very happy that you are aware that we live here even though you cannot see us; you have the faith to know that it can be possible for us to live in your garden and be a part of the community. It is important that humanity should know that we exist. So many children are told that fairies do not exist, although people buy books of fairy tales for them, and then proceed to tell them that we are not here once they get to a certain age. This is very sad, because children can often see us when the grown ups cannot, and they believe and have a faith that it is possible for us to live in your world because it is really our world as well as your own. We are quite an important part of it after all! However, we accept the fact that many people live their whole lives through without believing in us. That is all right, so long as some of you still have faith in us and believe that we are here.

It is rather like believing in God, is it not, because you cannot see God nor can you see the devas, so if you believe in God and in the devic kingdom, you can believe in us, can you not? Because we do exist, and are happy to live our lives out here in woodland areas and beside streams. We can live anywhere, but our favourite domains are in these country areas filled with beauty and peace, and therefore we are grateful to be here, and that this is our small kingdom. We give you all our blessings, and we hope that mankind will keep on improving in his ways, and allow the countryside everywhere, all of nature to flourish once again, wherever there has been pollution. We know that in time through people like you, it will become beautiful and flourishing once more. God bless, and farewell.'

This is Marcos once more. There is little more to add. I know that you are very pleased to have communicated with the little people, and now you look around with new eyes trying to see them. You can also see traces of growth that are peeping out from under the snow. You might think that this is a time when nothing is happening with nature, but you would be wrong, because there is much happening and the devic kingdom helps this on its way, bringing new growth to everything. Life is there, the sap is rising within each plant and tree, and soon that growth will be seen when the snows have gone, and the sun returns to bring new life to everything. All is very well, and you will find that everything will come to pass that has been promised to you, and within a very short space of time. God bless, Marcos.

COMMUNICATIONS FROM THE DEVIC KINGDOM 1
MELODION THE DEVA-8
(Target Wood, near Oakwood village)

My greetings to you both this day, this is Melodion, and it is good to be able to speak in this way to contribute towards the devic book, and I am happy to be among those selected. I hope that I will be able to contribute something worthwhile which is essential at this time of man's history. You, all who read these words are very conscious of the ecology at present. There is a fine balance between that which is good, and that which counteracts what is being done to help nature at this time. There is a band of people like yourselves who care for nature and the Earth, you know that the Earth is a living entity, and what is necessary is for it to be protected, nourished, and given as much help as possible to regain what has been lost.

The Earth has so many treasures, but man has ravaged the Earth in the past, and caused pollution and devastation of the forests over so many years, that the balance of nature has been upset more than ever before. However, this has been touched upon by other devas, and I do not wish to dwell on it, but I know that all of you will play your part in protecting your part of the Earth at all costs, and dissuading anyone that you encounter from damaging the Earth.

In the future, the Earth will gradually rise onto that higher dimension and is now, of course, you and the Earth are moving onto the fourth dimension and then the fifth. The Earth needs extra help which you are giving by directing the Christ Light into the Earth, all of this has been very essential over these years, and will continue to be until all have moved in that ascension process. Looking back on your lives, you realise that in the past, when some of you were quite young, the Earth had been protected and had not been so polluted as it has over recent decades. However, you can look back on those happy times and realise that they will come again, once the Earth has recovered from the onslaught of pollution, and your efforts will not be in vain.

We of the devic kingdom have been trying to nurture our territory and give extra power to the smaller devas, those who are in charge of separate flowers and plants. Wherever they have needed extra help, we have given that energy from our own reserves, so at this time we too are grateful for any help that is given. It is perhaps a nebulous thing to you, to think of energy being projected from us, but it is rather like radiation from the sun, that light source without which nothing would grow, and we have that energy within us, that similar warmth and light that we project towards the smaller devas and everything that is growing in this area of which we are in charge.

Nothing comes from nothing as they say, and you have to possess some form of power or energy to create growth. I know that you think of planting a seed and give it the right conditions that it will automatically

27

grow, but sometimes you will find that certain plants do better than others and you wonder why. It is all part of nature's way of protecting the strong, and the weak do not survive. So it is with us, we have to bring energy towards us from the realms of light, of which you are aware, but possibly not seen, unless you can remember what it was like before you incarnated, when you were 'home'.

Nevertheless, that capability is not always there latent, it is something that we have to learn to do from the start, that light which we bring down from the realms of light, and keep in within our capacity, because we do not have a physical body like you.

We are an energy, a centre of light, and therefore we contain within us what we bring from the realms of light, and if necessary we have to supplement this periodically, to preserve our power to be used for the benefit of our domain. All is light, and all is energy and life, that is what life is. The physical and the spiritual, it is all intertwined because those of you who are physical like yourselves are beings of light, and have that within and around you always. That light which has incarnated, the same light that has lived many lifetimes is there within and around you now. We of the devic kingdom are constantly aware of the light within each one of you, and we can see that coming towards us. We see your light more than your body because your aura extends around you, and that is what we tune into, the energy that is within you shows itself as light, and therefore we tune into that more than the physical side, and are aware of the brilliancy or otherwise of the light that is coming towards us!

Therefore you can be considered to be reasonably powerful, because we can see you quite clearly, and that light has been steadily becoming stronger over the years that you have been in communication with me, and those who read these words will be of a similar nature because all of you are light workers and are aware of what you are about in this lifetime, learning to evolve your soul that is progressing ever upwards, we hope. Over the various incarnations you have had, either on this planet or on another in the past, your soul has been evolving to be consciously progressing. It is something that comes from within, that hunger for knowledge, searching within and looking for, perhaps you are not quite sure what, but something that will satisfy the need of the soul, that knowledge, that ancient wisdom that has perhaps eluded you until more recent years.

Many people have been instilled with religions in the past that nowadays do not go beyond what has been known over the centuries. The churches have tried to modernise their services and attempted to bring them upto the level of those who have a broader outlook, but there is still that yearning for something more, and this is what you have been finding, that lost spirituality that has now been found. You will always progress from here because having awakened to that knowledge, it cannot sleep, and must continue to burgeon forth, blossoming like a tree that has puts out shoots, and then flowers in the fullness of time. This is what you are all doing now, you are blossoming, flowering and flourishing, and your souls are being nourished by this knowledge that you have received, and are spreading to others. That is your task in this lifetime to receive and pass on the words that are given to you from beings of light, many masters, angels, archangels and beings from other dimensions and space. You have accepted this as the truth, and it is the truth. All are working hand in hand for the benefit of the whole.

So that all beings, whether they live upon the Earth or other planets and stars, are linked together in a unity of minds and souls, and when the time comes for you at the transition into this ascension process, you will feel that you have come home. It will be more like the realms of light once this is achieved. Everything is working to this end and you have much to look forward to, and the truth is there for all to see. You will all achieve much in time.

God be with you all, Melodion.

COMMUNICATIONS FROM THE DEVIC KINGDOM 1
ASHTAR, SPACE COMMAND-9

My love and greetings to you this day, it is Ashtar who speaks, and I know that it has once been once that this channel has heard me briefly, but I am very pleased to be able to communicate with her and those who are interested in this work. All of you who have been receiving the words from the Masters, spiritual beings and those who join with me in space as you call it; all are part of the whole. We are not in little compartments, but all work together as one, combining forces against negativity and evil, and to benefit mankind and many other beings throughout the cosmos. We have been working together for many decades, and I know that you have read some of my words in books that have been channelled. These have been put together for a purpose, in order to lead humanity to a higher purpose within his life. To reach up to that higher level of consciousness, and to accept that what we have been attempting to pass on to humanity is the truth, all of you recognise the truth when you read or hear it. There is only one truth, and in service to God and all beings of light, we can only issue forth truth to those who will hear us.

As you may well be aware, there is an awakening within mankind at this time. These are the latter days mentioned in the Bible, and they are an important time, an epoch in man's history. You have chosen this time to incarnate and be a part of the vanguard to help to unite us in the work that we have to do together. There must be a large mass of humanity to sway the balance at this time of transition, for that mass consciousness is most important, to work against negativity in the Earth at this time. All of you are aware of the violence that has been flaring up throughout the Earth, violence with man against man. We look down on this and feel frustrated, and can do little apart from pouring down light, and hope that the negativity will gradually be overcome through the light from the Source, and from those of you living upon the Earth at this time, to help bring down that light into the Earth to spread it across towards all humanity. We have been working to this end for so long, and sometimes it seems that little progress has been made, but gradually we feel that the light workers have been infiltrating that light we have been pouring down, and using those energies thus formed to negate the violence, to bring forth positivity and upliftment, and generate that more freely. In time, all of you will find that your lives will be completely transformed.

Over these last two or three years there has been a general surge of activity with light workers in channelling words and light, those books that are in bookshops now are reaching out towards you. Channelled books, books about spirituality and many other subjects that are a part of the work in which you are actively involved. There are many books concerning healing, Ufology, Spirituality and similar subjects too numerous to relate, but are nevertheless subjects that were never written about a few decades ago. It was very difficult at that time to find books on subjects

30

such as are proliferating on your own bookshelves now. We realise that this awakening of mankind is self-generating and is accelerating, which is totally necessary. All of us who have been working towards this end are delighted that this is occurring now, because within the next year or two, it is most important that the mass of humanity is fully aware and ready to rise, ascend onto that higher dimension. It is time to begin, and the Earth herself is gradually being transformed.

Those of you who are sensitive to this will be aware of the continual speeding up of everything. Time is speeding up, people are generally more conscious of the ecology and change in climate. The seasons have altered so you would not have known what time of year it was unless you look out for flowers and trees, despite these last two winters. If you were to suddenly wake up after a long sleep, you might think it was midsummer, but it would only be spring. But many changes have occurred in this way, and the mass of humanity accept this and realise it is a change which is general throughout the whole Earth. Acceptance, faith and patience are necessary lessons to be learnt, and I think many of you have been learning these very fully over time. Perhaps you have had pain or disillusionment periodically, and this is all part of the growing process, which is part of the plan. You may look back on that time and realise it was just a step on the spiritual path that all of you are following.

There is great dedication and discipline within you all, and we are pleased that this is so, and we hope more will join in with this work all over the country. The words given to you by many channels and from many books are all part of the one truth, as I said, and mankind is ready to take his place and become part of the whole creation on a higher level of consciousness and being. There are others within the cosmos at a similar stage to you, and we are helping to bring you through that birthing process, re-birthing into the new. It takes time for this to occur, but have faith and know that you are all in the right place at the right time. We are very happy and delighted that you are aware of us, and know that we are here to guide you whenever the going gets rough. Be assured that we know how it is with you, and we give you our blessing and love, now and always. Believe me, mankind is ready to take that giant step forwards in faith. All is well.

God bless, Ashtar.

COMMUNICATIONS FROM THE DEVIC KINGDOM 1
MAGNUS THE DEVA (Kielder Forest) –10

I give you my greetings this day; this is Magnus. I know that you have attempted to reach me once or twice recently, but the weather has been against our meeting. Now is the time for us to join our minds together in true gratitude for being made of light and love, and for the knowledge that truth will be given always by ourselves to all who will listen. This is a place of true solitude and peacefulness, and has been so for many, many years; mankind has made little change to this area. Apart from bringing the water to many people, who have benefited from the reservoir, the area being flooded for that purpose, these forests have been undisturbed, apart from the occasional deforestation and replanting. It has an ancient air within it; the mossy banks and tree stumps make you feel that they have aged together in tranquillity over the decades. I am happy to be a part of this, and this is my domain.

Mankind has made his mark throughout the Earth over the aeons, but truly he will always only be a visitor here. The Earth herself is truly alive and well. She may be suffering at times from pollution through man's intransigence, but in the main, her arteries and veins carry very little pollution, if you consider the vast area of the Earth. Think of all the enormous oceans, lakes and vast rivers that dominate the planet. There is much more water flowing over the planet than there are continents, and although man has created pollution, and attempted to assuage the Earth by clearing it from time to time, there is little than man can do to stop the Earth's progress. She will continue despite anything that is done to ravage the planet. She will always continue, and everything that lives upon the planet is governed by the Earth and what she provides. The Earth, the mother, Gaia, always provides for all life that lives upon her.

Man finds it necessary to provide his own sustenance despite the Earth's prolific fruitfulness. There are always things that man needs that are not necessarily natural products from the Earth herself, even though there is much provided for him, and even though he feeds off animals and birds besides the natural cereals, grains and fruits of the Earth. Mankind has much, and has done much both for the Earth and all that dwells upon it. Perhaps there has been much criticism of man, but he has provided for his kind over the centuries, even though pollution and some devastation have occurred as a result of some of this production. Nevertheless, natural products such as coal and oil have been taken from the Earth and used for the benefit of man over the past centuries, and without which, transport and manufacturing could not have taken place. Many things have happened over recent centuries, but this past decade has seen a change in man's development.

People like you, on the path of spirituality have begun to truly awaken to that inner knowledge, that inner peacefulness and a new outlook on life that could never have been achieved without turning within.

Meditation has changed those who are awakened, and there will be no turning back for all of you on that pathway to evolvement of the soul. In past lifetimes, you have all been experienced in working in temples and other places of worship, and throughout history, many of you have formed groups who have been either monks, priests or priestesses, and been able to learn from the ancient wisdom that you have within your souls. It is all there within you. You do not need to look far, or even delve into many books. You have within you all that knowledge that you have gained in those past lives, and achieved much, and it is all surfacing now. Now that you have awakened to your souls, or higher selves, that wisdom is beginning to unfold again, and you can just wait for this to occur over time. What is time? It is nothing to us, and is completely invented by man, and therefore what we might consider time as perhaps an hour or a day, a hundred years or more, could have gone by in man's conjecturing. But nevertheless, gradually mankind is learning how unimportant time is.

But the most important thing is his soul and the way he reacts to people. The most important and powerful tool that man possesses is love. Love creates and concerns itself with others. It is something that comes from your very heart and soul. If you do not have love within your heart, you can do very little in the way of feeling towards or for others. It is necessary to have that love which you can project towards all with whom you come in contact. It is even more powerful than thought, and thoughts can create and cause good and evil. Thought comes first, and then deed follows; sometimes you do not need words, but the thought and the love are the most important within a lifetime.

Try to develop that unconditional love. It is not easy; nothing is truly easy in an incarnation. It may be easy at times to laugh with people, and this is very good medicine for all of you, laughter has been called the best medicine, and in truth this is so. Without a sense of humour, and love within you for others, life would be extremely dull, painful and lonely. Always remember this, and try to think of those who are alone and do not have such humour in their lives. It is a very important part of life.

Expect nothing from others and you will never be disappointed! That is also a very true saying, and it is always a great pleasure when perhaps something is given to you, or you are asked to join up with people to do something which you had not expected. An unexpected spontaneous outing that does the heart good. These are things that help to make life more interesting, and you know these gestures help to enliven life. They may be simple, but they generate the love and happiness that is an important part of life's experience. The true experience of life is that of learning, loving, being and doing. You notice how the order comes; doing is the least important, perhaps, unless it is doing something to help others. It is rather like healing, there are many who can heal, and others who are just on the point of learning how to heal and send out light through themselves to others. Without love this cannot be accomplished. So always feel that love towards another, otherwise than healing cannot take place, you can generate energy, but not truly heal or help. Healing can be on different levels and not necessarily what is wished, but it can be given despite the fact that the cure may not appear. It may not be that person's karma to receive true healing, but nevertheless, if the wish and love is there, benefit is given, on a different level through the spirit, from one soul to another, and the light that is given, that healing light is always beneficial.

I do hope that my communication to all of you has been of some help. It is always difficult to say from the heart what you feel through another who is channelling your words, but I think that I have conveyed my meaning and love towards you all.

I wish you well, and am happy to have contributed to this book.

God bless, Magnus.

COMMUNICATIONS FROM THE DEVIC KINGDOM 1
ARCHANGEL RAPHAEL –11

Greetings to you all, this is Raphael. I am so pleased to be able to speak through a channel because I have rarely spoken, unlike Michael and Gabriel. Perhaps I am more reticent in communicating verbally with humanity. There are certain channels who are used regularly by me, but not so generally, I usually address those who are working in healing capacities, and it is pleasant to be able to speak to those who normally have not been in communication with myself. I am always regarded as the healing Archangel, and truly this is so. My energies have long been pouring down upon humanity, and other beings throughout the universe, that you see above you when you stand outside on a starlit night. There is much of the universe that you are aware of, unseen partly because, of course, in the southern hemisphere different stars are seen. When you are gazing upon them in the northern hemisphere they are below your horizon, naturally, nevertheless, all are present and many are inhabited by beings different from yourselves, as you know. However, they too require healing light from time to time, some not as frequently as those on your third dimension, but occasionally that healing light is sent out onto the higher dimensions.

Of course, the bodies of humanity are changing now, and have been for several years, gradually raising onto the fourth and fifth dimension. It has been a slow process to begin with, but then it will suddenly change, so that you become aware of many beings on other dimensions, who surround you at present, but are unseen or unheard by most of you. I say most, because some of you are extremely sensitive, and can see these beings occasionally. As they are on a higher dimension they move extremely fast compared with humanity, rather like the little people whom this channel will be bringing through before the end of this book. They also are part of the devic kingdom, and help to bring forth their essence towards many growing things, and so they too are a part of the healing process in nature.

I am in great demand, shall we say, at times of war upon the Earth, and as there have been wars and rumours of wars throughout man's history, my healing energies have been used very frequently. I have healing angels who support me in this work, and they too help humanity constantly. Of course healing is essential at all times, and it is not just at times of war, when surgeons are operating, or when there are accidents of all kinds, healing takes place constantly. There are certain times in your life when you are aware that healing has helped you through a bad time. As you know, everyone benefits from healing throughout his or her life. It may be necessary to heal a wound, or a mental or spiritual hurt that cannot be seen, but is there within you, when someone wounds you through words or actions that are thoughtless, so we are always present to help humanity and others in this way. Of course there are those

35

including some amongst yourselves who send out healing using the Christ light, from the Source of all being. That Total Light which you as light workers have been aware of, and which is accessible to all if they know how to use it wisely for the benefit of suffering, both humanity and all the other kingdoms across the face of the Earth.

Healers of all kinds, both doctors and nurses, and those who use natural healing, the complementary methods of healing rather than the allopathic medicine, all are included in the generic term of healing. All use healing light, whether they are aware of it or not. The energy that is essential for the purpose of healing is pouring down constantly. As you are aware, there are many energies that pervade the Earth, and of course this includes the negative energy that has been generating itself as a result of that group within humanity that is evil or violent. Those who profess religion, but use it against their own people in order to obtain power, and everything that is negative us caused by the need for power, and the greed within those who are generating this negativity. These elements of violence still abound on the Earth at present, as it has been said by others that this negativity will escalate before light and love negate this and overcome it. It will be at that time that the complete change will occur, the ascension of man onto that higher level of being that has been ordained for him for many years and is taking place.

Many changes have happened, and I am pleased to say that once this level is reached, there will be no more negativity and evil upon Earth. It will be entirely obliterated, especially when the photon belt appears. It will be a cleansing on the Earth. It will come, but as you know, it cannot be seen by ordinary eyes or even through extremely powerful electronic telescopes. These new scientific instruments are capable of seeing much more than was ever seen in the past, but nevertheless, they cannot see onto a higher dimension. Therefore, those who operate them can have no warning of when the photon belt is appearing to surround the solar system, but in time it will come, and these changes and healing will occur upon the Earth and to all that lives upon it. So when that time comes, and man comes into his own, it will be as was prophesied, there will be a new Heaven and a new Earth, so the Second Coming will occur. This may happen before the photon belt appears, because increasingly more of you are able to bring through these communications that are from the realms of light, and so it will be that man becomes his higher self, and therefore will in future be able to bring through communications from within constantly.

This capability is gradually spreading and accelerating as man becomes more spiritual in his nature. It is there within all of you, as you know, and will generate itself so that you all become one with the Source of all. I will leave you now with my blessing and hope that man will become a Christed One, a Master in his own right in time to come. All is very well, and that healing and divine light is spreading throughout humanity. God bless, Raphael.

COMMUNICATIONS FROM THE DEVIC KINGDOM 1
ACHILLION THE DEVA (Swallowship Wood) –12

This is Achillion, my greetings to you all. I am pleased that the book is now being completed and that I will be able to conclude everything that has been recorded previously. I know that all of you have the ability to see that the Earth is troubled at this time, and we will not dwell on that subject any more, because all have had their say, and all the devic kingdom, concerned as they are, wish you well. There is so much to include in this book, and I realise that not everything has been encompassed. One of the kingdoms has been somewhat neglected, that is the mineral kingdom, and you only have to look beneath your feet to see that the whole Earth is composed of minerals. The absolute core of the Earth, the structure of the Earth and all upon it is based upon the mineral kingdom. Think of the mountainous areas, great canyons of the Earth that are all composed of mineral. Many mountains in certain areas of the Earth are comprised of rock because they are so high that they are above the tree line, and therefore denuded of any vegetation.

The mineral kingdom has devas within it, of course. They are not so well known as those devas for each plant, flower and tree, as well as the landscape angels, of which I am one, and so progressing upwards to the archangelic hierarchy. Nevertheless, the devic kingdom is not fully represented unless the minerals are included. Within each crystal that you see, quartz for instance, each crystalline structure has within it a small deva who is in total charge of that crystal, and if you use crystals you may be aware of this. I am sure that most of you have used crystals in some way, though they may not be used for healing. Perhaps you have them throughout your house, and if you are aware of their activity, you will realise that they are important to safeguard any radiation coming from computers or television screens. They have many parts to play nowadays, with their inclusion in technology, however we will not go into the scientific use of crystals, only the fact that the devic kingdom consists of mineral, plant, and of course ourselves.

Everything is linked together in some way. Throughout the whole of nature, all the kingdoms of the Earth, everyone and everything is linked to the cosmic consciousness. Everything is one, and that whole consciousness is where man returns when he leaves each incarnation. We of the devic kingdom are, of course, a part of that consciousness, and therefore those who can link with us can consciously link with that universal mind. It is a part of everything that is alive, every being within the cosmos is linked to that consciousness, and therefore you realise that there is no separation. Every being, humanity included, is a part of that whole, and can link with the Source of all whom we serve, and are consciously aware that our life is one of service, both to the Source and to all nature. The part of nature that we undertake to take care of, is what we live for, and those small beings who are serving us, the Landscape Angels, are also serving that Great Creator, the All That Is, the Source of all being, whatever you wish to call that great energy that provides everything for all beings.

We have said previously that we are fountains of light of many hues, so visualise yourselves, if you will, as you can be seen by us. You might think that you will be seen physically clothed with material garments, but we see you as you truly are, lighted beings. Particularly those upon the spiritual path who are attempting to bring down light, and serve as light workers naturally, you have brought down light into yourselves, and this is now a part of your auric field, therefore your auras are shining even brighter than previously. So much can be told from a person's aura, how they think and how they feel, and how they are physically, so the aura is a great indicator of that true being within the physical body. Eventually, when you manage to achieve that higher vibratory level, you too will be able to see one another's auras, and know if the person you are talking to is truly as honest as they appear to be. Some attempt to cloak their feelings or thoughts, and they are the ones you will be able to discover whether they are perhaps not always telling the truth.

It is difficult I know, because sometimes truth can be harmful if you are truly honest with someone and don't tell white lies at all, and then the truth can be a little hurtful at times! I mean generally that you will be able to see one another's truths, and in fact how each is feeling, because if you are feeling well and strong, your aura will shine brightly and extend well beyond you, so that your aura and other people's auras beside you will be intermingled. It would particularly be so with someone who is a very evolved soul, such as Sai Baba or Mother Meera. These are true beings of light whose auras can extend across miles to include all mankind and living beings, because they are beings of bliss and love. They are extremely powerful; the power of love can be stronger than anything, so that if you will use the light from above, and the love from your hearts, you cannot fail in the work that you are doing serving mankind and the Creator.

We truly look forward to the time when all of you will be able to see us, the devas, the angelic kingdom, and of course includes the little people, who are very shy and hide from view, although sometimes they can be seen fleetingly, particularly by children, and children truly believe in them when they are young, and we hope that the little people will not be too shy today to speak.

Little People speaking: - We are here! We are here! It is so good to see you, we have not spoken to you for so long and we knew of your coming through Achillion, and although you have never seen us, you have been hearing us for some years now. You believe in us. This is Olivia and I know that you are aware of my colour, that shade of mauve that is so delicate, and which you searched for in your clothes to try to link with me in some way. You have the scarf which has that colour in it, but you, Beryl, although you have not seen us, you have shown my photograph to those who are interested in us and this is good, because

38

then in time you will be ready to see us once you have reached that higher vibratory level. Some who are spiritually aware can see us from time to time, but others like you can hear us, and in time will also be able to see us, and we too look forward to that time because we wish to be part of your group of world servers.

We too, play our part here in our domain, and we are proud of our surroundings. They are beautiful are they not, with all the flowers out at present, the colour of which is the colour of my robe, as you know. These rhododendrons are wonderful flowers and they attract us to them. You may not see us, but we are here surrounding you, some of us landing on your shoulder or looking straight at you, and sadly you cannot see us but you take our word for it that we are here. This part of the countryside near streams and woodland is where we usually have our territory. All of us are working together for the good of nature, linking with the small devas of the flowers and trees, and of course with Achillion who protects us all, and links with the Source of all being. You link with the light and bring it down into the Earth, and to all who need the light given to them for healing or comfort, and this is good. We know that humanity is working in this way for the good of the whole, and we are pleased that this is so, and that more and more are becoming aware of this capability, that they have always had, but not many were able to use it. We wish you well and we know that you have to leave us, but we are pleased you came, and we give you God's blessing. Farewell....

All of you know the power of positive thought and that linked with the light can be transferred and used for many purposes, as you know, for the good of the Earth, healing, upliftment of someone who has negativity within them. That positive thought can counteract the negativity, and bring about a complete change, generated through the power of thought, light and love. Love is the most important of all, that power of love without which healing cannot take place. As they say, 'love makes the world go round', this saying could not be truer, the power of love, thought and light gives instantaneous healing and upliftment.

Remember that you are most important within the Earth at this time; this incarnation is truly a most powerful one to be used for the good of all, because all of you have chosen to come now, you are all awakened beings with evolved souls, and you have the power to awaken others, and this is you allotted task to help to awaken those who have also chosen to incarnate now, but have forgotten why they came here. You are among those who are here to help at this time. All is very well and we are very happy to link with you in this way.

God bless, and keep you all, Achillion.

39

CHANNELLED COMMUNICATIONS FROM THE DEVIC KINGDOM

Book Two

BERYL CHARNLEY

CHANNELLED COMMUNICATIONS FROM THE DEVIC KINGDOM
Book Two

CONTENTS Page

Channelled by Beryl Charnley

COMMUNICATIONS FROM THE DEVIC KINGDOM 2
ACHILLION AND FRIENDS, SWALLOWSHIP WOODS-1

Welcome to you both this day. I see you have brought your new small instrument with which to record my thoughts. I am sorry you are not all present, but next time I am sure that you will all be together. Strange isn't it that this is the first time you have been barked at by a small dog, the very first time you have your instrument with you!

You were talking previously about beings living within the core of the very Earth herself, yes that is right, well, as your daughter said, they are at a different level of being from yourselves, and could very well be living in a different state. Not physical, but spiritual in the fourth dimension, which eventually the Earth will be, and this is so. I know you thought it strange, and could not picture how they would emanate from inside the Earth, but if you think of them as being on a different dimension, then anything is possible. You have an open mind, and therefore are ready to accept it, but wish to have confirmation of it first. There are more things in Heaven and Earth as they say. So that is a new thought to be aware of that there are beings living within the Earth, the centre of the Earth, on a different vibration from yourselves, and yet part of the Earth itself. Strangely enough, now that you have the benefit of your machine, we have not got on to a long train of thought. It is to be one of those days when you are frustrated in a number of things. This occurred with your recording today, and it seems as though you are going to have a number of people disturbing you on the walk, but never mind, it is good practice to try and work on two levels one after the other.

Yes, wherever you look ahead, behind and around you, for that is my territory. I am the Deva of all the land that you can see and beyond, as you discovered when you went to the other wood and found that I spoke to you there too. There are many nature spirits and little people who work with me and for me, for the benefit of this area of the countryside. In the hierarchy of Devas of course, I am just one of many thousands or more within the realm of the British Isles, and of course, if you multiply that by the number of areas within the world, then I am just a number, but I serve the Earth in my capacity, and am proud to do so. When we reach the lower wood, perhaps the little people will have something to add, because what they say is of interest also. I know that in the future, you will have much of interest on these small tapes from the various places that you visit, even across the world if you take this with you in your holidays, as I think you will. So, in the pinewoods of Yugoslavia, you may find a different nature of Deva, of a different name completely from my own. The Devas keep in contact with one another throughout the world through thought. Yes, we do link together, particularly those within one country, but there is a network across the world, and they combine together to help to benefit nature of all kinds, particularly if there is some tragedy such as a forest fire or a flood, and they can attempt to help that area by uniting together in the work at hand.

You know that when you went to Yugoslavia before, there had been forest fires raging or smouldering over the months, whilst you had been having a large amount of rain in your country. It seems strange that with so little distance in-between countries, there should be such a marked difference in climate. The balance of nature is a very delicate problem, and the scales can easily tip one way or the other, and if this occurs, it must be rapidly put right, because if the balance was in any way badly upset, the Earth herself would suffer, and all upon her as a result. This has happened from time to time as you have heard in the legends and stories of the Flood, which certainly were true, and they have been passed down in different folk legends, and indeed of course, within the Bible as it is the truth. The various versions all blend together to make the one truth. I will now leave you and see whether your small friends join you within the lower wood, I will rejoin you later, farewell.

Ah! You are here again to join us, and we are here to greet you! We are pleased that we can voice our thoughts onto your machine. This has never happened before, and it is quite exciting! Now then, what can we say to you to make it of interest to other people? We are the spirits of the water, and of the woods, and we hope that mankind will be good to us. We watch his ways, and know that people such as yourselves would not harm their surroundings, but there are many who do, and who ravage the Earth by devastating forests, and this results in making deserts of places that were once thickly populated with trees and vegetation. Please stop them because the Earth needs help at this time, and we must do all we can to avert any tragedy. Also, why are people so cruel to animals? They do not realise that everything is one, and if they hurt one thing, they hurt everything. We of the woods and streams appeal to you as our spokeswoman for this work. Perhaps this is a way of getting through to other people, and reaching out to those who do not understand. I do hope so, we all do, because our surroundings are so precious to us, and we know they are to you and so many others, who enjoy the nature that surrounds them.

The beauty is all about them, but so few have eyes to see it. People walk past with their heads down, looking where their feet go, but they do not look up at everything that is around and above them. The sunlight filtering through the trees, and even in the winter, in the depths of the snow there is beauty. This must be preserved for all time, and for all men. Please pass these words on to others that they may heed them, and take action upon the words. Remember the Earth and all upon it are man's responsibility, and although we work to preserve all the structures of the Earth, all that grows, and the waters that flow upon it, mankind is ultimately responsible to God. If you look around you, you can see what man has done to this forest, some of it has been completely devastated. We hope that it will be replanted and renewed. We suppose that a lot of it had to be cut down or fall down, but so long as it is replanted and brought to new vigour, then no harm will be done. It is when man cuts down forests and jungles, and they are not replaced, that the balance of the Earth is tried very sorely.

We do not wish to be sad, as by nature we are happy, we are just concerned. Nature is burgeoning forth as you can see by the buds, and we have been doing our part in helping this to occur. There are even small leaves on some of the trees, and a lot of the flowers that have come out early this year, have not been hampered by the snow and frosts that we usually have in this part of the country, but the river as you can see is quite full with all the rain. Still, it is better than snow. We will walk with you until the edge of the wood where Achillion will rejoin you. "Thank you." When you look back on our talks together, I hope you do it with affection, yes I know you do. We enjoy talking to you, and we have been pleased to add comments for your machine. We hope it will be of value, and look forward to your next visit when we will have more things to say.

We hope you will soon find that place of peace that you are looking for. I don't think it will be too long now, and then we can come and visit you in your garden. There will be others who live there permanently, but we can always come and join them temporarily, just to speak to you. "That will be nice." There are several of us here, including your friend Olivia, who is on your photograph. I am Janus. I know that I am not the one who spoke to you before, but may name also starts with a J. "We are very pleased that Olivia could show herself on the photograph. We hope that some time in the future more of you can do so." Yes, perhaps we will, but it will have to be Heather's camera. Hers is superior to yours and can work at a faster speed, which is what is necessary, so that we can show ourselves. We will do our best for you, we promise. We will say goodbye to you here, and will see you next time you appear, goodbye, God bless. "You too."

Your friends had quite a bit to say after all, which was nice. Now you have the bird song behind you on the tape recorder. You are being sorely tried today. (Sounds of people nearby). Great Beings who overlight the whole world are helping at this time as you know, to raise the consciousness of all upon the Earth, and we hope that in some way we also can do something towards this upliftment. You see around you all the beauties of nature, and it is hoped that everyone will take their part in attempting to preserve these beauties as they are, and restoring them to their former glory; for more and more places that have been ravaged by man are being replenished and brought back to their once beautiful conditions. If you could look down on the Earth as we can, and see it as those above you can, then you would realise the importance of all this. I know that you do, but perhaps are unaware of the overall picture of the Earth and that nature must be balanced all the time. You have seen in nature programmes on your TV, how old trees make way for the new, and so long as that new undergrowth and saplings are allowed to grow unrestricted, all is well, and all will be restored.

The old always has to make way for the new in every aspect, as in other aspects of nature. It is rather like mankind, the old dying and the new being born. Not necessarily new spirits, ones who have lived before in other times, returning to help the world at this time. Those who are being born at present will have much to teach their parents, because they should be adapted for the new way of life when the Golden Age comes, as it will. Spirits in these newborn bodies are shining forth, and we can see them and they are a wonderful sight. Some unaware of their 'trailing clouds of glory', but many who have been aware from the beginning, will continue to be aware of their spirituality the whole of their lives. I do not have much more to say now. We have almost completed the tape, and this has been very pleasant talking to you upon your machine for the first time, and I hope that in the future, I will have increasingly more to tell you; the words of wisdom that I may have, and which others may assist me with. It is not always just one who speaks, and can be one who is the spokesman for a group of other spirits. As you heard from the Archangels Michael and Gabriel, it was not always them as individuals who spoke to you, but spokesmen for them. You can understand that such vast Beings could not always be there in person. Well, I think I have completed all I have to say for today, so I will say farewell to you both, and good wishes to Gordon, and hope that I will speak to you again soon. God bless.
Achillion.

COMMUNICATIONS FROM THE DEVIC KINGDOM 2
ACHILLION AND FRIENDS, SWALLOWSHIP WOODS-2

You must always keep that sense of wonder in your minds; that wonder that is like a child's, and rather like the animals too. They have a sense of wonder when they find somewhere new, a sense of excitement, and think of newborn lambs at play and the joy of life within them. As you watch these two dogs playfully running amongst the woods you realise what a difference there is between yourselves and them. You are wrapped up in your physical bodies, and as you age, the excitement begins to pall, but perhaps within you there is still that child that senses these things, and is aware of what is around you, wishing you could see the spirit world and the fairy folk who live here. All of us are present, and yet you do not see us, but you all have open minds, which is most important.

I, Achillion, greet you all this day, and am very pleased to see you together, because I know that you have great work ahead of you, which you will forge between you. A new life which will spring from your oneness and from the home that will be a centre of light in the North. It will be a most important one, and will serve everyone who comes within range of it. There will be many who will come for help and guidance, and also for healing of the mind, body and soul. This is something that is required by all, as you know who are ready for this healing at this time before you begin your life's work, and there are still many years left to you, and this is the most important task you have undertaken.

I see within your minds many seed thoughts and glimpses of what you feel may be in store for you. There is a certain state of excitement, and a sense of a new beginning, and this is so, there is always excitement when a new step is taken, a new road lies before you, and you know not precisely what you have to do, but you will be given guidance when the time comes. The fact that you saw someone twice, or thought you did, shows that 'there are more things in Heaven and Earth' you might say. You do not know which one was the real one, or whether in fact she and the dog were really there, do you? Both of them could have been spirit, also you do not know whether other people saw them, it could be that you were the only ones who did!

Nevertheless, these things do occur from time to time just to show you that all things are possible. Perhaps one day one of the little people will show themselves to you. You already have one on a photograph, which is proof to you that they are all around you, living on a higher vibratory level than yourselves, and this is why it needed a high-speed camera like Heather's. The speed is all-important, and this is why it is rare to see one of the little people, it is only when they choose to show themselves to you, and this occurs very rarely. They have to slow down their vibratory rate in order to appear to you in this way, so, very few people are able to see them. In time to come, when you are working together, we will be here always if you wish to speak or listen to us. There will be a Deva wherever you live, because we overlight our region of the Earth, and although it may not be myself, it will be one of my friends and your friends in charge of your section where the house in which you live will be situated. The little people who have said that they would visit you will certainly do so, and be sure that there will be others in your garden who will commune with you in time to come.

Some of your work will be with the Devas, and in fact we will help you in growing all that you wish to grow within the garden. I think that this has been done several times before, and the first that was known I think, was in Scotland. The first that you heard of, at Findhorn, where we worked in conjunction with all the people who lived there at that time. Since then I believe it has changed, but there are Devas still helping them, though not to quite the extent they did when the first vegetables were grown there. It was proof that we were indeed working hand in hand with those who founded Findhorn. There will be others who will come and join you from time to time, who will help you in the work that you are about to start. There is another who is waiting to join the four of you, he does not know he is to be part of a group, but he feels that there is something waiting for him in the future, and he knows he has work to do, but is not absolutely sure what it is to be. He has an open mind, and will be only too pleased to work with you; he too will do some channelling work similar to this.

Yes, as I have said before, as far as the eye can see and beyond, is the area of which I am Deva. Of course there are so many other Devas, as I have previously said. I am just like a cog in a wheel, but nevertheless, our function is important to the Earth and all that lives upon her, and the Earth being a living being herself, needing all the help she can get at this time. Man in particular must help this living being to survive and to be as she once was, full of glory and beauty. The part in which you are walking is beautiful and full of green shoots, leaves and flowers, but there are many parched areas throughout the globe that are devoid of beauty that was once there. This is due to a change in the climate that has come over the Earth, partly due to man's work. With his cutting down of many rain forests, this has resulted in the deserts that are forming that were once fertile plains. We know that there are many of you that are aware of this danger, and who are doing all you can to keep this within people's minds, always remember and remind them, that things could be better, and mankind must be responsible for the Earth and all that lives upon it. He is the guardian and should be working with us to preserve all that lives upon the Earth.

Yes, the more you look at nature, the more you realise how much is overlooked by mankind. So few take the time to study their surroundings, and all the little things that are beneath their feet, which includes the business of ants and bees going about their work. All these things are a part of man's inheritance, and yet even the very animals are threatened at this time, with the roadways that man is creating, cutting through the natural countryside, and leaving so little room for the animals that would normally live in it. The birds too need their natural places in which to live and breed. It is important that these areas are kept sacred for them. Many waterfowl have been thankful for the work that has been done by far-seeing men in the past, and we hope in the future. I will say farewell for the time being, and allow your small friends to join you in the lower wood, and I will return later.

Here we are! We have been waiting for you to arrive and we are waiting behind each tree for you! We keep it secret where we are hidden, so that you do not know where to look! Yes, we are full of mischief and fun, but we are pleased to welcome you here to join us at this time, and perhaps one day you might have a glimpse of us, just perhaps if you wish it! You are dressed in the colours that we like, vivid greens, reds and yellows, we love these colours, and we are pleased to see that you also love them.

As you know we are part of the forest, and some of us live within the waters that you now hear, others are behind the trees and within the cracks of the bark. We are elfin folk and we work to help nature in all its ways. There are so many of us here watching you. You would not believe how many of us there are, but we are so pleased to welcome those who are in tune with us, those who believe in us and would wish to see us one day. As a result, we congregate and watch you as you arrive to join us, and although you cannot see us, you can hear us, which is the next best thing. Once within our woodland walks you are in an enchanted area, a place in which anything might happen, it is a place of peace and tranquillity, and yet of wonder. We welcome those who wish goodwill towards nature, and those who live within her.

We, the little people realise that you have many demands on your time, and yet you give time to come and visit us quite often, and although, as I said, you cannot see us, you can sense us around you. There are many who watch you from the other side of the water, who live within the hollows around the rocks, crags and tree boles. This is a place of beauty on this day of sunshine, and yet there is much that is dying as you see, the trunks of many large trees are lying sadly in the midst of the wood, and yet beneath the other trees there is new growth.

It always springs up ready to start a new life similar to man, the old makes way for the new. Babies are newly come into being to start a new life, and they may have lived many times before, and have great knowledge within them once they become able to express themselves at an older age. Mankind can choose to serve us and help nature, and we know that you too agree with this thought. Nature is bounteous if it is allowed to live normally, the vegetation and everything that grows upon the Earth will respond, if given the right conditions. The warmth of the sun as you see it today, and the rain all work together to make a beautiful picture, and help all growing things.

You are finding it a little more difficult with the presence of the little dogs, but never mind, it is good practice for you in concentrating on what we are saying, while watching the dogs at play. They are full of excitement, exuberance and fun, and we enjoy them around us, and sometimes they sense us here. I think the one beside you knows I am with you; she has her ears pricked. Yes, this is a very busy time for nature. Everything is beginning to spring forth in abundance, and many creatures are busy searching for food for their young, both animals and birds alike, insects also are making their own homes of varying kinds to produce the young. We help them in our way, as we help with growing things, and the sylphs of the air too join us in this work. We are all around you, love is all around you, and we give out our love towards you and all who accompany you. Until the next time we meet, we give you our blessing.

You are indeed blessed this day, how hot the sun is now. It is a beautiful day for the time of year. April, as you have discovered can be a very varied month for weather. Hot one moment, then freezing, then hot again, but so long as that prevails you will be content I am sure. There are many things that I would like to speak to you about, but at this time there is little tape left on your machine, so there isn't time to give a discourse on any lengthy subject. I hope one day perhaps, when you are alone, to get on to something more serious. Something that appertains to the work you have before you. You will be told of course by your guide Tomas, but I too have knowledge of what you are about to undertake, and I know that you all wish to serve the Lord in whatever way you can.

Once this decision has been taken, opportunities present themselves to you, and you find yourselves thinking in a different way to what you have done previously. There is so much knowledge to be gained; so much you have been reading about that previously had been unknown to you, but nevertheless is of great importance to mankind, and we hope that in the future this knowledge will be passed on to all people.

You are from the Source of all things, all are one, everything that lives is part of the whole, just a different facet, and you are part of one facet. All these facets of the jewel of life combine together to serve God, and I am proud to do my work as another facet of the whole, serving with the Devas to preserve nature at all costs. I give you my blessing upon this day of beauty, and look forward to your next visit. Blessings to you all this day, farewell.
Achillion

COMMUNICATIONS FROM THE DEVIC KINGDOM 2
HELARES, JUGOSLAVIA-3

There are many who linger here from the world of spirit, but it is not they who speak to you but we of the trees, of the winds and of the sea, who attune to you on this beautiful morning. We are happy to greet you, as I know you are happy that we can commune with one another. We have at times spoken to you since you came, but we knew that you were not quite ready to receive our communications. It takes a little while to become adjusted to new surroundings and to unwind, as you call it. On board ship when you came to the island, we spoke to you, and you were so happy that you could understand us, and of course, as I said at the time, thought is universal. It is immediately translated through your own mind. Thought can be in any language, as you know God speaks to all, and there is no need for translations of any kind, and we, the Devas are the same. It is Helares who speaks to you, who spoke to you on your short walk to the little pavilion, and you wished to know my name. I know that I hesitated before I gave it because names are of little use to us, but we know that you find it important as a reference, but you will understand in time how unimportant a name is in the world of spirit.

I now go through your mind and remember what was said to you when the Archangel first spoke to you. He called himself 'a winged one' and this is true, because they have wonderful fiery wing-like structures surrounding them. They are magnificent, and if you were to see an archangel, it would be difficult for you to put into words, therefore winged one is as good a name as any, but then you desired to know who it was, and although you did not ask, you wondered, and you wondered if you were imagining all the words that were given to you. Naturally this does occur because when such communications begin, it is a difficulty that has been faced by many in the past. Over the many centuries of man's existence there have been those who have been called upon to transmit our thoughts to others, only those who will accept the truth for what it is. As they say, truth is stranger than fiction, and the thoughts that are being given to you from us who are of the Devic Kingdom, have been given to others in the past, and in the future it will occur constantly, because it is necessary for mankind to know how we care for him, and how we wish to commune with him. We have communed over the centuries as I say, and sent our thoughts to mankind, so he knows that he is cared for and guided through his life, although many may not be aware of this.

Life is all part of God's experience. This may sound strange, but through man, God lives physically. That divinity within each one of you is part of God and His Plan, and you are fulfilling your part of the Plan in accepting the responsibility of attuning towards us, and transmitting our thought to others. It has often been thought that those who can attune to us are strange and not quite of this world, but it is the others who cannot hear us who are strange, shall we put it, because all men have the capability within them to attune to the Devic Kingdom, to their guides and to God Himself. There are so many who are unaware of this, and sadly it seems that we have only a bare minimum of humanity with whom we can commune. Nevertheless, those who accept this can transmit it to those who cannot hear us. We hope to have several transmissions while you are on this island, and we will continue later with this one. You may have a rest where there is more breeze, as the sun is extremely hot, and don't wish you to burn, so we will say farewell for now.

When you return to your woods at home, you can picture this beauty, similar in a way to your own favourite wood, but nevertheless there is an essential difference. The warmth in particular, and the variety of trees, although pine of a sort, like your larch trees at home, there is a difference. Your climate is so different from this country's that it takes some time for you to adjust, both physically and mentally, the heat affects you in both ways, particularly those who are sensitive. There are many who can switch from one country to another without feeling any difference, apart from the warmth, but there are so many different aspects physically, emotionally and mentally that you may have noticed that this adjustment takes a few days, and now I think you are fully adjusted and ready to accept our communications to you.

There are those whose books you have read or are reading, who have been aware for some time of their spirituality. You may have been aware for many years of course, that there is a spiritual side to man. The development of this spirituality is a different thing, the learning of all different aspects on esoteric lines, metaphysical, and the very essence of divinity. Man has great capabilities to learn constantly, the whole of his life. The essential nature of man is such that he can prove to himself each day, his capability of uplifting his consciousness to a higher level. You now understand why men become recluses or hermits. It is to get away from noise, pollution and other people who are obtrusive to their attunement to our world. This is why the ideal place for this work is in peaceful secluded surroundings, which is what I know you are hoping that your next and last home will be.

As you may have noticed places of this type are rather rare, particularly in the areas you have been searching, but one will be waiting for you not long after your return home. When all is ready for you, the time and the place will be right. Everything is cared for all your lives, if you give your lives to this work, then at the right time, the place will be found for you. You are ready now, both of you, to do the work that you chose to do before you incarnated, and as a result, everything will start from a new beginning. You will be guided through what it is you have to do. Do not concern yourselves with small details; everything will come to you in its own time. People will come to you when you are ready and not before, so do not worry that you will not be capable of coping with what it is you have to do. When the time is right it will happen and not before. We are aware that you do not wish to become recluses as such, but to be in an area such as this, a place of peace away from the madding crowd is something you had not dreamt would exist, and yet throughout the world it does, and people are capable of living in these conditions. They have never known anything else, or they have chosen this situation, well away from main areas where people pass, and so are content.

In the past, philosophers such as Plato in Greece, and more recently Nietzsche, Jung and many others have studied the human psyche, particularly Jung, who was extremely sensitive and experienced in his weighing up of mankind through dreams and thoughts. These men have been aware of their ability to communicate with us. Perhaps their method of communication was different, each person after all is different, but the end justifies the means, and in whatever way the transference of thought from the Devic Kingdom or from God has been given to them, they have passed on this knowledge through lectures, and in the writing of books. In the future this will continue, but more and more of mankind are developing the ability to channel our thoughts as you are doing, and perhaps this is something that will be of more benefit to mankind? I do not know; it depends on the ability of those who can achieve this attunement, and whether they are able in their own way to communicate these thoughts to others of like mind.

Naturally, philosophers have very intelligent minds, and the capability of passing on their knowledge to many more people than the normal man in the street. Nevertheless, man has the capability to find a way to pass on these communications to others, and in various ways this has been done over the last few years, so that many more people are becoming aware of spirituality rather than spiritualism, which has been frowned on in the past, but spirituality is a completely different facet of the whole.

Many have been concentrating on life after death instead of life after life. Think about it and know that of course this is the truth, which so many have overlooked, or perhaps not been aware of it. Those who have concentrated on spiritualism have often been unaware that life after death leads to more lives, more incarnations, and that the soul has lived in many previous lifetimes before this one, experiencing many facets of spiritual and physical life to make up the whole. Looking back on a lifetime of experience, you may begin to realise that much of that experience has been purely physical, emotional and mental, but not particularly spiritual until recent years.

There are many such, although there are some who from very early years are spiritually aware, but they are in the minority. In the main, people begin to have an inner life when their families have left home, and they have a little more time to contemplate and meditate in peace. This is the time when the fullness of life comes upon them, and they realise that there is more to life than they have previously experienced. Philosophers such as Jung were aware from an early age of their inner life, therefore, these particular men have been endowed with qualities that perhaps set

52

them apart from others, and in so doing, they were given more time in which to live their inner life, and be aware just being, instead of doing all the time, reflecting and dreaming.

Dreams are important, and an integral part of the spiritual and physical life of man, and must not be neglected. There is much to man that he is unaware of unless he is fully integrated in all aspects of his life. Most people imagine that dreams are just nonsense, and quite often people think they have not dreamt and not remembered, or they have thought so little of the dream that they have not bothered to recall it. This is rather sad, because dreams can show and reflect what is missing, or what is important in that life. They show the inner life, for they reveal what cannot be shown physically or by speech, in other words, they are quite an important part of life itself, and this is sometimes a new aspect on living, because so few people take much notice of their dreams. There is so much for man to learn about himself, and others, and this is a way of learning. Recalling dreams or thoughts that have passed into the mind and out again almost without recall, but if these thoughts and dreams are written down, they can be remembered, and there can then be a better understanding of that person and how they feel. What is missing in their lives, or difficulties they are passing through, as shown by these thoughts and dreams.

Everything must be recorded as a whole, because man has many parts. There is the obvious physical side of man; there is his mental attitude to himself, to others and to all things. There are also the emotions, and all these parts combine together with the spirituality to form the whole. The holistic approach, and when man recognises his divinity, and realises that he is responsible for his own life, then that is good. This must occur within the lifetime, or else it will be wasted, and have to be learnt in a further lifetime. I will say farewell for now, we will talk again.
Helares.

COMMUNICATIONS FROM THE DEVIC KINGDOM 2
HELARES, YUGOSLAVIA-4

You have within you capabilities of which you do not know, but on the other hand, if you knew everything in advance of it happening, then perhaps it would give you cause for thought and unnecessary worry, because all these things happen at the right time, when you are ready for them to happen. Remember you are capable of anything with God's help. This is a place of great beauty is it not? What a wonderful sight to have sea all around you. Something you are not used to, and yet it is something inbuilt in man to appreciate the splendour of the sea and its power. Yes, it is Helares who speaks, and those who surround you who you cannot see are the sylphs, the elves and undines, who are watching from the water. Yes, you think how wonderful it would be to see them, and perhaps one day as you have been promised, you may.

You have already seen one little person on your photograph, and it would be a very good idea to have a camera capable of fast speeds, to capture more of the little people who can show themselves to you, if they wish. We hope that on your trip tomorrow to the island that it will be a day of beauty and sunshine such as today. Yesterday's rain has renewed everything. Every so often the parched earth needs rain to bring nutrients into the soil, and so transmit these to all the growing things that you see around you. All these flowers are truly beautiful, because no one uses anything to destroy growth, nothing that is not natural. Sometimes fire is used to try to destroy some of the tree stumps and this type of thing, but apart from this, everything is as it should be in its natural form, unhindered by the pesticides that are used in your country.

There are many creatures that are perhaps frightening to you, but they mean no harm. They just like to examine everything within their vicinity, to make sure that it is nothing that is edible, but in the process, perhaps they might frighten you, such as the snakes you have seen. They are harmless though, and just like the other insects and flora on the island, they are indigenous here and do not mean any harm. It is just their strangeness to you that makes you feel frightened. As ignorance of anything brings fear, so it is with these beautiful creatures that might have been worth photographing, such as the metallic beetle that you are staring at so nervously. They too have their own beauty, and look alternately bronze and green. However, this is by the way, it does not appertain to any teaching, apart from the fear that comes through ignorance. Thought comes in waves, and this is just a time for a pause in my considerations.

There are many things to learn in life, and as you have been told, change is one of them, because it is through change, either in being transported to another land, or change in the conditions and situations of life, that lessons can be learnt. Many consider that change is bad, and they hope that things will continue as they always have been, but this cannot be, for there is always change. It would not be natural to continue always, year after year, without change of some kind, and through this, lessons are learnt. Think of the seasons, they change constantly; it would not be natural if they did not, because through this, new life springs up and the old makes way for the new. So it is in everything, and you are coming to a point in your lives when there is to be change. This is good, because your plans are to work for God as much as you can, and always remember that He works with you through others. Others who help, the Messengers of God, He is omnipotent, and yet it is seldom that He speaks to man. It does occur of course, but in the main, His Messengers speak for Him.

You have timed it perfectly so that we are not interrupted this time, as you were the first time constantly, through people coming past and the occasional noise. The only noise that you hear at present is the sound of the sea, which is lovely, and it is something you have longed for, as you never normally hear at home since you live in the centre of your country, and the sea is a long way off. You have nothing of this description anywhere near you, and therefore the beauty is boundless to you. This country is a dramatic one, with its beautiful mountains, the wooded slopes coming right down to the rocks on the seashore. It is something strange and alien to you, and yet beautiful. This headland would be a dangerous one to come close to by boat. That is why the fishermen leave their nets along the shore that you have just passed, but this headland is a beautiful point in which to see the ocean surrounding you, and today is perfect for this purpose. All around you are little people who support me in the words that I say to you. There are those who spoke whilst you were on the boat, and who welcomed you to this new land. We hope that you will continue to enjoy the beauties of this nature, and the wonderful butterflies that you see before you, with colours that you have never seen before, like floating flowers!

In your life's work you will be serving God and man in the best way that you can, and that is all that is expected of anyone, and in this you will be fulfilling your task on Earth. Once you have set your feet on the road to truth, you cannot turn back. This is something that you know in your heart of hearts, and once the mind is awakened to its spirituality, you realise there is no turning back, only a furtherance of this knowledge, and you feel you cannot learn enough, you cannot learn it quickly enough!

There is so much to know, so many facets of the whole, so many facets of the oneness of all creation. Knowledge that all is one, all life springs from God, the One Source of all, and we are all a part of that in whatever branch we take part in. Whether in the physical life or the Angelic life, all serve God in their own way. We in the Angelic or Devic Kingdom do not have free will such as man has, but we are ordained by God to serve Him, and we do in happiness, and will always continue to do so, and serve man also. The nature kingdoms are a part of our natural work, but this work also brings us in touch with humanity, therefore all are linked together by our Devic Kingdom. The interlinking of all the natural kingdoms is part of God's Plan, and he hopes that mankind will develop this capability of linking each kingdom together through us, and of course, through Him.

It is hoped that mankind will understand this interlinking, and realise that he must protect nature. He is the one after all, who is incarnating and therefore the one who must be the protector of all. So it is that man must shoulder his responsibilities, take on the guardianship of the Earth, and all that lives upon her, and through this the Devic Kingdom can work, linking man with God and all that lives upon the Earth. The beauty of nature is there for all to see, and all that you see around you is perfection, or it would be perfect were it not for man's traces around you. The rubbish left behind, sadly by those who don't care for their beautiful surroundings, and drop all manner of paper and plastic articles that show how uncaring in general mankind is for his beautiful surroundings. It is mainly thoughtlessness and ignorance that causes this. He must be made to realise that he is the one who is endangering the species of so many flora and fauna, not necessarily by the rubbish and traces of what he leaves, but by the pollution that is much worse. Fortunately for this island, pollution is something that is not apparent, and it is so peaceful here.

As you have been told, it is unnecessary for law, the police to be present, for this is something that is most unusual to you, and you are happy to learn it. Life is safe and pleasurable in such surroundings. All you can do is marvel at the beauties of nature, remember all this, and keep in your hearts and minds that simplicity of the little children you saw today. 'A little child shall lead them' are the words that you know, and this is the truth, because all you need is a simple mind and heart to follow where God will bring you.

Pollution is a serious threat within this world, and if man is not careful, much of the Earth will be despoiled, but if more will learn that theirs is the ultimate responsibility, then perhaps they will allow nature to remain as beautiful as it is here, and not allow the Earth to be polluted, as it is occurring throughout so much of the world. The Devic Kingdom in your country have already warned you of this, and how man must be responsible, we are so aware of what is happening. We can see it happening throughout the whole of the Earth, and are in touch with other Devas naturally in our work, and help in times of crisis. Sometimes it falls upon us to band together to help nature in fighting something that is polluting or despoiling it, such as fire, another hazard, particularly in this country at certain times of the year when rain is scarce. Sometimes there is pollution of other kinds, but we of the Devic Kingdom do our best in trying to make man aware of his responsibilities through the many channels that are beginning to spread throughout the globe.

You have read some of the history of the islands, and you know that man has lived here for many centuries, and yet there is very little left, apart from ruins here and there to show how many thousands used to live here. So it is that some things may seem strange to you, demonstrating that man has left his mark in some way for a particular reason, quite often

56

to bring fresh water to this country. Large cisterns of water exist near the harbour, as you know, and there were other areas that were used, other villages throughout the island that no longer exist, because nature has taken its toll and covered most traces of man's existence. As you know, there were many marauding pirates who attacked the island over the centuries and that is why the fortifications were so powerful. The village as you see it now was much larger in the past, and all the inhabitants could be contained within that fortress at the monastery, which is in ruins, but still shows its fortified walls. Time has changed the way of the inhabitants of this lovely island, and it is mainly fishing, tourism and a little agriculture that is the way of life here now. Times have changed and are peaceful once more.

As time progresses, change at the beginning is something in which man learns to face truths that otherwise he might turn his back upon, and therefore it is necessary for change to occur, so that man will learn through this. I think that today's teaching will be a little shorter than the previous one that overran slightly, as you know. It is sometimes difficult to judge whether the last sentence will fit into a tape that is so small. I say teaching, for want of a better word, it is a communication between us, and I hope we will have several more before you return. It is pleasant to be able to speak to one who can hear me so well and appreciates it, and is sensitive to the finer feelings of mankind. I hope you will return along this path once again, because it is an easy one for you, not too hilly like some of those you have tackled. I wish you both a happy day, farewell for now.
Helares.

COMMUNICATIONS FROM THE DEVIC KINGDOM 2
HELARES, YUGOSLAVIA-5

Good morning to you both. I knew this as a place of peace and solitude, and therefore this was where I chose as being the best for us all. I am surrounded with the little people, and maybe they will be wishful to speak to you later on, and they support me and we speak with one voice. (Yes, the seagull also speaks to you!) I wish to speak to you on many things, the oneness of man with nature and all beings. There are links from man to God, and from God to man, we are one of the links in the chain, that chain that unites us all from the Source of all things. As you know, there are many worlds and universes, so as you are aware of this, I will not speak of such things, but let it be known to others that they are but motes of dust in the sun's rays, although all are important to God, so do not belittle yourselves in that respect. Just know that you are important to Him, however tiny you are within the universes, and therefore you must keep that upliftment of mind and know that He is dependent upon you, despite your small part within the universes. The part that man must play is to keep his mind and consciousness uplifted, to as high a level as he can maintain, reaching ever upwards throughout his lifetime, to know that he can be one with us and hear us whenever he can.

Each man and woman should keep that consciousness to a higher level than the physical, lifting upwards towards spirit. We of the Devic Kingdom know that you meditate and this is good. Meditation and prayer are all-important, but we are aware that man must live his life upon the material plane, and therefore, for the most part he cannot spend his life attuning to us, unless he lives as a recluse. Each person must play their part in whatever way they can, and if you can spare more time uplifting your consciousness and channelling our thoughts, this is all to the good, because this can be passed on to others who do not have the time that you have. I know there are demands upon your time as well, but perhaps in the future, in a few years time or less, you will be able to spend increasingly more time in meditation and prayer, and in helping man to link with us.

We hope that more channels like yourselves will continue to spread throughout the Earth, because it is essential for humanity to recognise the fact that the Earth must be cared for and treated as a living being, which is what it is. If man goes too far with his nuclear experiments, then he will be shrugged off like an insect upon someone's arm. The Earth must protect herself, and this is how it will be done if man goes too far, and God recognises this fact, so man will be given warning through the channels so he can alter his ways. This must be kept in your minds at all times as it is the truth, sometimes the truth is hard to bear, because although you would not offend nature yourselves, other would. So, warning must be given and spread to those who will accept it, and perhaps

58

there may be one or two prepared to spread the word to higher levels, to those who govern the major countries of the world at this time.

When you look back on your small beginnings in these channellings, I know that you marvel, because you had not expected anything like this to occur in your life, but as I have said before, if you knew in advance what was to be, you might have turned aside from sheer fright, and this would never have occurred. It is a subtle process, and your capabilities are extending slowly but surely, and you are gaining confidence in speaking our words and thoughts that are dropped immediately into your mind, as though they were your own thoughts. This is as we would wish it, for we do not insinuate ourselves upon you, you are ready to accept our thoughts and take heed of them, passing them on to those who are interested. There will be many who will reject these thoughts, and some may consider, but forget them. Always remember that nothing is said without reason by the Devic kingdom, your guides, or indeed by the Christ. All are working towards the same purpose in extending man's capabilities, and bringing forth his resourcefulness and power to help all who are in need of this help. This includes the planet Earth, and all that lives upon and within her.

You see around you some of the flora of this island and how beautiful it is, we hope it will remain so. Islands like these are few and far between, where man has left very little of his own traces upon it. There is no pollution from traffic or pesticides as I said, and therefore it is hoped that this will spread further afield, and in the future man will use other means for transportation, because in time to come resources will diminish, and be extinguished. Man's nature is creative and in the future a means of transport will be found that doesn't need any fuel. I think this has been told you before, but I reiterate it because it is of great importance. There are those who are scientific and inventive, who are even now working on this, and in time it will be developed, and there will be no need for noise and pollutants in the atmosphere. In the past this was done when man first originated on the Earth, and much occurred in those times that have been lost to man, but we hope that he will relearn these capabilities and know that it is in his power to do so. You are impressed by the beautiful butterflies that you see flying past you with their many hues, well, man could fly like that if he learnt the secret, not exactly in the same way, but with very little effort. There is that ability of learning to transport himself by other means, and it will happen in time. Make the most of your time here, and remember my words and the beauty of nature surrounding you. I will say farewell because there are others who wish to speak to you for a short time. Thank you for your time, it has been pleasant meeting you both. "Thank you."

We are here, hidden from your view, but nevertheless there are many of us surrounding you, and we greet you on this beauteous day. We have been watching you and know you would not hurt anything around you. We are pleased about this because there are many who would pounce and kill just for the sake of it, and also others who might do so through fear and ignorance. We know that given the opportunity, you would marvel at us and our many friends who live in the air and sea. You look around you but cannot see us, nevertheless, just accept that we wish you well, and are very happy to be able to speak to you with one voice. "May we know who is speaking?" The one who speaks for all of us is Otto, I have been named the spokesman, and I pass on our thoughts to you. Be gentle in your attitude towards all creatures, whether they are living plants, insects, birds or animals, and stones, everything has a life of its own. I think you know this, but we just hope that man will continue to change his ways and be thoughtful for everything that grows on the Earth. We have our work to do, and although it is not as important as that of the Devic Kingdom, nevertheless we are busy in our own way, putting essence into the flowers and plants surrounding you, which you have been admiring, and we are pleased that this is so, because it is our life's work.

We are like the butterflies and fly wherever we wish. We can escape from the Earth's gravity and lift ourselves at a moment's notice, faster than a butterfly, as you know, because only once have you captured one of the little people on a photo. We know this from your mind, and we are pleased that you have actually seen one of us, because no matter what man may think, we are here. We exist in many forms, and the one you saw was a small fairy. Many of us, like myself, are elves and gnomes, and of course there are many forms that we take. There are those who exist in hearths called salamanders, who help fires to burn, undines who live in water, and sylphs in the air, so it is with us, and we know you are aware of this, and hope more will realise it is the truth. Now we will let you continue your walk, and just wished to speak a short while to let you know we are here as well as in your own woods nearby. We exist all over the Earth, doing our work secretly, silently and steadfastly. We wish you well, and hope you enjoy your visit.
God bless, Helares.

COMMUNICATIONS FROM THE DEVIC KINGDOM 2
MELODION, OAKWOOD WOODS-6

Greetings to you both, this is Melodion. I am pleased to welcome you to our haven of peace. As you will have noticed, very few people come this way, but we saw you approaching and were pleased to see you were returning so quickly, and both of you are extremely welcome. You both like water and love the sound of it. There is more sound today because of the rain, since Beryl last came this way, you see I know your name, but then of course, we know many things from your minds, apart from anything else. Minds are very interesting, because we can search through and sometimes find a little piece of information that is missing, that you might want to know out. For instance, you have been talking today on the teachings that were being received, and mentioning that there was a great deal of repetition. This is true, but it is nevertheless necessary in certain respects because without repetition, you would not realise its importance, and sometimes something has to be repeated as it hinges on many topics, it is part of life's pattern. Perhaps I am not making myself clear, if this was not repeated, then it could be difficult to explain certain aspects of daily life and its spiritual side.

Man can take many paths such as the one you have been looking at, wondering which way to go. If he takes a certain path, then it leads him astray at times, as you were led astray the last time you came here, and found yourselves lost. This is why you were deliberating as to whether to turn at that certain point, and this happens in a lifetime also, as well you know. Certain times within a life you have the possibility of changing in midstream, taking a turn and moving in a general direction, either with the crowd or away from it, and at this time you are deliberating as to whether to live in solitude or live near other people. If you go into complete solitude, it would mean you would help less people in the work you are doing, but if you go into an area where there are certain habitations, and you are not too far from those you have been meditating with, then they too can join with you in the work you have to do.

If you decide to take a turn further away from them, then you would have to make the decision to help another group of people, and an entirely new section of the community in which you would be moving. This is the difficulty in finding a place away from sounds that might disturb you, but sufficiently near for those you feel drawn towards, and still enjoy your company and the work you are involved in. It is a difficult decision, particularly so as there are very few properties available at the moment, but we know you are in God's hands and He will look after you when the time is right. At present it is a little early, wait a little while and all will be ready for you. You must have faith, and patience, because these are necessary for everything that concerns you, both in searching for the property, and in the work you are to do, to serve God and man.

You have turned aside from the main path, and I think you will find this glade will suit your mood; it is very tranquil and quiet. Feel the benefit of these beautiful pine trees around you; absorb the atmosphere and strength within the trees. They are here for the benefit of man in many ways. Man plants and grows them to maturity, and then cuts them down to sell for various purposes, but in the meantime, if more people knew of the benefits of pine trees, they would come amongst them and absorb their quality and life giving vitality. As you know, pine woods have a definite quality that is unlike any other type of wood. It is in a way similar to the quality of air on a hill or the seashore. All these places are ones that can be peaceful if you are on your own, but they have a certain benefit for man. The wood has changed considerably since you came some years ago, you are thinking to yourself how completely different everything is. The beech trees that your daughter drew and painted seem to have disappeared, but it is just that you are in a different area, where you went to previously has changed and is more overgrown, therefore this path draws you towards the coniferous part. Go up to the right, and you will perhaps find the area where you walked before. This clearing has been made for the benefit of vehicles to reach parts of the wood that could not be otherwise accessible to them, in order to carry the logs down to the road.

Nature is very prolific, and at times it has to be kept down for the good of either a garden or a wood, and at times it seems sad that trees have to be cut down either for the benefit of man or as a means of thinning out, but sometimes that has to be done, and do not feel that it is wasteful. Just apologise and say, "I am sorry but you have grown in the wrong place", if a tree that you do not really wish to have in your garden suddenly appears. Therefore I think you will understand that the tree will accept this without any undue worry on your part. If you still feel badly about it, it is possible to replant the tree in the wild, and I am sure it would take if it is still small enough. Otherwise, do not concern yourselves unduly if you have to thin out trees that would otherwise normally grow in the wild. Remember that you can always ask us anything that you wish to know, particularly regarding nature. Nature is boundless, particularly in areas where there is plenty of rain, and you know that you are all right because here it rains a fair amount, but in places that are hotter and drier, it is more difficult for nature to survive. Green growing things find it very hard to gain a foothold that is really firm, unlike the grass, trees, shrubs and flowers around you. Therefore, be grateful and realise you are indeed fortunate to be living in such an area. Most of the British Isles is lucky in this respect, and particularly those in the south benefit as a rule from warm weather, but the climate changes have occurred throughout the globe.

As well as the climate changes there will be more powerful changes that will alter the whole of the globe. This is the general teaching at this time, to prepare humanity for these global changes in climate, and to prepare him for something that may be worse if man in general does not change his ways from violence. It is hoped these changes will not be too catastrophic, but by the time you have settled into your property and begun your Light Centre you will have realised it will be your last move, and you will find you can manage to cope with any change from that particular place. We promise you that it will be a place of beauty and peace. Just have faith and know that the property will appear at the right time.

The friends that are joining you in this venture are searching in vain for that which they seek, but if they can possibly hold on a little longer, their property too will come on the market. It is more difficult in their situation I know, and it is hard to promise something that doesn't seem to be forthcoming, nevertheless, I say to them also, have faith and know it will come to pass when the time is right. You will all look back on these months in time and realise the time was not as long as you thought, that the waiting was not as bad as it appeared to be, and it was well worth the wait. Always remember the poem by Rudyard Kipling containing the phrase, 'If you can wait and not be tired by waiting'. Read and absorb it, and remember he must have experienced those particular problems in his life, as do most people at some stage. It is difficult when you cannot see very far ahead; but perhaps these words will be of some comfort to all of you, to know that in the future, the near future, you will find what you seek. At times you wonder why difficulties rear their heads constantly, and you think; something else to worry about, but there is usually a reason.

There is much to be learnt as has been told you before, through difficulties and experiencing different situations. Perhaps something you never experienced before, but something that had to be, you may have had it too easy for a while, and this new lesson had to be learnt to give you an understanding of what others have to experience for much of their lives. I cannot tell you the reason, nor can I really help you, apart from these words of comfort and truth, I hope you will return again and maybe you may have some news, good news by then. There is still some unfinished business is there not Gordon, and it was prophesied that when you business was completely finished, fast on its heels would follow your place of peace. Well, remember these words and do not search for something that will not appear until the right time. That is all I have to say, and I hope it may have been of comfort. Well, I wish you farewell and I hope you will return again soon.
Melodion.

COMMUNICATIONS FROM THE DEVIC KINGDOM 2
BEOWULF, LADY'S WELL-7

I wish to welcome you both to our beautiful haven of peace. It has been pleasant over the time that I have been in existence, and it is improving as man is making his mark upon this forest. I have been here for many centuries, and cannot tell in your time, but I am the one who contacted you previously, Beowulf, yes it is the same. This is my territory, and I am happy to be the spokesman of this area. You have contacted many of my kind since last we met, and I am very pleased that you are able to put down my thoughts within your machine.

I hope that man, as all the Devas do, will continue to improve these areas, these parts of the country where animals and birds may live in peace. So much of the countryside is being torn asunder by roads and places where people can live, it seems that there are increasingly less places for the natural indigenous wild animals of the country to dwell. I hope that mankind will remember this, and realise that he must keep clear sections of the country for this purpose.

Your mission today is one of goodwill and blessing upon the sacred place nearby, and I know that it will be a day that you will remember, because you will take some of the Holy Water from here to other places, other parts of the country that need to be re-energised, and need help, and through meditation, prayer and invoking God's blessing, this can be done. I am pleased that you are to be one who is doing this work, and to be able to keep contact with you in this way, so I am sure that we will meet again.

Now you have reached the place that you were searching for, and the Holy Water is nearby, and you can create your little ceremony of peace. You have already greeted me who am the spirit of this place, all we wish you to do is to kneel and pray, and God will bless this place.

The blessing you received was from the Lord, and if He is to guide you, then your footsteps will be true and sure, and you will be bringing His Light and Love to all the sacred places you visit. You have our blessing to both of you this day, and to your husband who waits for you, Godspeed.

I think you have now regained your breath after walking up the slope. You are now approaching the second sacred site you are visiting today, the Drake Stone, and are planning to implant four of the pebbles that you have picked up both at Simonburn and Lady's Well, and to sprinkle the Holy Water around the stone to revitalise it for future years. I give my blessing to this sacred place, as well as that of our Lord's.

Well, you have duly fulfilled your mission and carried out the task, of blessing that sacred site, despite many people around, you managed to do it quietly and unobserved by others, I am glad that this is so because these sacred sites are in need of help. The next one you go to will be much further south and you will have another Deva who will guide you on your way. I give you my blessing once more, and wish you well on your

64

future journeys, and I am sure we will meet when you return for more of that clear Holy Water from Lady's Well. Godspeed and farewell, Beowulf.

COMMUNICATIONS FROM THE DEVIC KINGDOM 2
MAGNUS, KIELDER FOREST-8

Yes, this was the first magical place, where the little people spoke first, and you feel that now you have returned, they may be ready to speak to you again. This is Tomas at present, you realised that it was my signal for you. Wait and see what occurs later on by the stream, and I think you will find there is more inspiration there. At present you are waiting for something to occur and usually it occurs when you are least expecting it, and this is the best way for things to happen in its own good time. Part of your spiritual unfoldment began when you first came to this place, a side of your spiritual development that you had not expected. There are many facets to the whole, and people only understand what they have come across. So there are many people who would not believe that such a thing could occur, mainly because it had not occurred to them. It is only through experiencing attunement to all facets of the whole that you can understand, and understanding is a large and important factor in man's development, either spiritually, mentally or physically. Understanding comes from experience.

Yes we are all around you. You were not allowing us to come into your mind, as you were on a higher level of spirituality, and have just closed your eyes and become aware of our presence. You dare not open them in case our thoughts disappear, and perhaps with closed eyes you might see us, because you cannot see us through your own eyes at present. Perhaps in time you will be able to, and then how wonderful you think it would be to see just one of us, the little people. In our many guises, fairy folk, elfin folk, sprites, sylphs, undines and all the Devic Kingdom, there are so many of us. You cannot imagine the multitude that dwells within the countryside. There are some who are able to see us, but very few, and in fact you are one of the few who can hear us, and be sure that it is us and not coming from your own mind. You know that you are not thinking these thoughts, and therefore you are aware that we are speaking to you. We spoke to you for the first time at this spot, and we are pleased to welcome you back. We realise that you can record them on your little machine. How wise of you to bring it with you when you knew you were visiting this area!

You ask who it is who speaks, well, I am one of the elfin people, and my name is Truton, yes you have not heard a name like that before. We have strange names compared with your own, although I know that you have found a little fairy who showed herself on a photo, I get this from your mind, and she is called Olivia, and from your mind I can see her on the photograph. You see, all things are possible, things you would not have believed, but you are learning, and we are pleased about that. When you look back to the day when first we spoke to you, you have done much since then, very much on a higher level of existence in your mind, but always remember that we love to speak to humans, those who believe in us. Try to pass on this knowledge that there are such people as ourselves. I have been pleased to speak to you, and hope that you will return again. I know that you plan to go by the stream lower down, and we will inform our friends there to be ready for you when once again you can hear thoughts from the little people. Farewell, go in peace.

We of the woods and water greet you. We are happy to meet up with someone who believes in us, and can hear us and will perhaps see us in the future. I am sorry that it is not as sunny and warm as it was higher up, but sadly it is a day of mist. You were fortunate that the sun came out for a little while, however, we wish you a warm welcome to our domain, and hope when the weather improves once more, you will return to us and allow us to speak our thoughts though you. Our friends in the section of wood several miles back informed us that you were on your way, and that you would be getting to us within a short while. We hope that man will do his best to restore this beautiful planet to better conditions, and that mankind himself will improve. There are many of us here who hope that this will be so, in fact we know it will be.

I have taken over from the little people, and my name is Magnus. I know that perhaps this sounds a Viking name to you and it is so, and I am in charge of the Devic Kingdom in this area. The one who spoke to you when you first came to this spot spoke as one of the little people, and then he passed me on. It is better this way, and then you do not hesitate, you continue on the same way. You have improved immensely since the little people first spoke to you several years ago. It must be about five years perhaps. I do not remember in time, in your years that are different from our time. Time is relative, and only exists for man; in our world time goes on indefinitely like an endless belt, extending into infinity. But I was talking about mankind, and saying that in the future, conditions will improve if good overtakes evil, and those who are on our wavelength shall I say, help conditions.

Try to put their views and our views to the governments of the world, and attempt to uplift the consciousness of all mankind to make men realise what they are doing to this beautiful planet, with pollution and cutting down of trees. There is a natural time for all vegetation to come to an end, to die and make room for new growth, but at the moment there is very little new growth-taking place where beautiful forests are being swept from the face of the Earth, and soil is eroding, and the climate continues to change. The climate is all-important to the Earth herself, and to the peoples upon it. Realise this, and I Magnus predict that the sweeping changes that will occur will be for the better.

Man is beginning to think, and think on a more definite line, a line that he must pursue. It will help all living things and improve the situation that is insufferable when you think of the rivers and oceans that at present are getting worse every year. Something must be done very quickly now, otherwise all the sea creatures will die out if man continues in the way he has done over the last few decades. He has been allowed to get away with murder, of many creatures that have been in existence since the Earth began. Many of which man has never seen because they live within the oceans of the world, but they help to balance nature, and the conditions of the water and land, and if they are wiped out, then the whole balance of nature will suffer. Man must realise his responsibility as guardians of the Earth and act swiftly. Try to be a spokeswoman for the Devas and for the Earth herself. It is most important that things are altered before irrevocable changes take place. We think that your government is beginning to realise this, and we hope that the governments of the whole world will participate in working together for the good of Planet Earth.

Gaia, the Earth, is a living organism who must protect herself, and if change becomes too great, then man himself will suffer. I do not wish to be negative, and be a bringer of bad tidings. I only wish to help, and if more people were able to be in contact with us, then more could pass on this message, so I am taking the opportunity of speaking to you, so that this important message can be spread to others of like mind. We are very happy to greet you this day, and for you to take away our strong feelings about Earth, and the conditions upon it, and we hope that before too long, changes will occur which will improve the Earth and all that lives upon her. We know that this is in your heart and mind, and those of your friends and family who think in a similar way. We bless you and we hope that you will help at this time, passing on our wishes. We know that you will do what you can in your own small way. Whatever you can do we will be grateful to your for this. I, Magnus, give you and you're my blessing this day, and hope you will return. God bless.
Magnus.

COMMUNICATIONS FROM THE DEVIC KINGDOM 2
ACHILLION AND FRIENDS, SWALLOWSHIP WOODS-9

I, Achillion, greet you and am happy to see you all today. We have not seen you for some time, but we know that you have been otherwise engaged, particularly down south in Glastonbury where you recorded a message from St Michael. We know this from your memory. We see and hear things from you that you would not imagine, and we know that you met someone while you were away who could see me, and also see the Yugoslavian Deva from your mind. I know it surprises you that such things are possible, but you must realise that as life progresses, you will discover more things are possible, that you would not give credence to, or would not have done ten years ago, but life is like that, if you continue the learning process. I know that many at your age think that once you get to fifty or so you stop learning, and just persevere with what you are interested in, reading anything you feel inclined, and give up learning anything, but that is not the way of life. Life is given to you for a purpose, and part of that is to continue learning right until you pass into the spirit world. If you live a full life, that is what is intended, then the learning and experiencing always go on. Your main purpose in life, your most important task has only just begun, so there is much to do for all of you from this time onwards.

I know that what you had hoped for has not come to pass yet, but it will do. The prediction is still correct; perhaps the time was wrong, and not meant to occur when you and we also hoped. There are reasons for everything, and the fact that the business deal did not go through, meant that there was a hidden reason for this. It could be anything from the timing of your purchasing a property to the wrong person taking over your business, who knows? It is in better hands than ours, and we just hope it will not be too long in your time, and the sequence of events is still to take place. I know it has been a tense time for you, but when you look back on your whole life a few months is very little when you think of it. The main purpose of your incarnation of serving God has yet to be fulfilled. You have begun with this task, but it will continue, and will take more of your life, and a great deal of time, but time which you will feel is justified, and you feel is worthy, and I know that the work you undertake will be graciously received.

We know you had a message on tape last night through Tom, and tonight there will be more, it may be that you will work together, just wait and see. All these technological miracles can help things to occur that would not normally have been recorded in the past, particularly our talks within the woodland areas, where you normally would have to carry heavy equipment do this work, but now you can carry this little light instrument with you, and we can communicate with one another, so that my talks to you can be passed on to those who may be interested in anything I have to tell you. In future times it may well be that mankind will work closely

69

with the Devic Kingdom in order to bring about a balance of nature. Nature requires help at this time, and requires man to change his attitude of mind, so that the Earth can be restored. There is much for mankind to do in certain areas of the world where drought, famine, and flood have been occurring.

This part of the world is relatively trouble free, but there is still much for man to understand. There are places that are being swept aside, natural habitat of your indigenous wild creatures that have been cleared, and will never be the same again unless man restores them. But this will not occur if new road systems are continually being made, and wide tracts of countryside spoilt for the sake of speed. Transport is expanding daily, and in time to come there will have to be sweeping changes because in the future, fossil fuels will dry up, and there will have to be alternative means of transport. So man will have to change his ways drastically, when that time comes. However in the meantime, it will be interesting to see whether there will be a change in man's attitude towards nature. We hope that you and others like you will be able to pass on our anxiety to those who hold the balance of power. I will leave you for now and allow others who may be waiting to speak to you, farewell.

Yes, we are here! We have been watching you for some time, your friend has been aware of us. We like to see who is coming before we speak to you, and we are very happy that you have come to visit us again, although we know that so far you have not seen us. Yes, we are taunting you again I know, but perhaps one day, especially when you have your camera, the new one that will be able to follow our speed. We are on a much higher frequency than you are, and as a result we have to slow down our voices and our rate of movement in order that you might see us, and this is why it is so seldom that anyone is able to do so.

We know that you met someone while on holiday as has been said. We see it in your mind, and she has seen some of our little people, our brothers and sisters in another country, and she was able to see in your mind who had been speaking to you while you were on holiday. No, there is no such thing as time, not in our way of thinking or living, but we know it is important in your lives. We understand this, but we cannot really appreciate it. We live so much longer than you do, and therefore there is time for everything that we wish to do, but we know that you are limited in many ways, including movements, which are so slow compared with ours, but we know that you are not capable of moving any faster, and we know that your finest athletes, although very fast compared with most people, are desperately slow compared with us, which is rather interesting, but we do not compare our selves with you, and we are happy to greet anyone who wishes to be in touch with us, and try to understand our ways.

You can hear the water in the distance where you always used to think there must be many elfin people living, but now you know we are everywhere. We could be behind this very leaf that you are passing, or fluttering above it because you cannot see us! Nevertheless, we are here, and there are many things that we wish to communicate with you and others like you, so you understand our way of life. At this time of year we are helping all of nature to come to a close, and gradually bring within themselves the very essence of their life force. To gradually withdraw that and keep it inside the trees, shrubs and all plants, ready for the winter months, so that all is preserved for the coming spring. Who speaks to you today? It is Janus, and my companions are with me. "Hello, we are happy to greet you, all of you." There is much to see that is beautiful in this area, and we are very fortunate to live here. You were in a place of beauty yesterday, and our brothers and sisters who were with you there spoke to you, also the Deva of that area who has been in communication with Achillion since. So many people do not really appreciate the beauty of all the seasons. Soon there will come the time of hibernation for the animals and insects, and everything that lives in this forest will gradually grow more dormant through the winter.

At present it is a place of beauty, with all the colours of autumn, but soon all the leaves will fall, and the branches and twigs will be bare, and then our work will gradually recede, giving us a little time for ourselves to do what we wish, and we do have time for amusement in our lives, because so much is packed into one day, compared with yourselves where everything moves more slowly. We are rather like butterflies, who flutter quickly past on a summer's breeze, colourful as flowers. You are wearing the colours we like, vivid and bright as in a child's paint box. Some of the replicas that people have in their gardens of garden gnomes we laugh at, because they do not resemble us in many details. Perhaps the colours they are painted, but the size and shape are rather varied, and do not resemble us in any way. Perhaps some of our older gnomes look like them, but mainly we do not look like that at all! It has been pleasant talking to you today, and we send our greetings to all who are interested in our words and work. Farewell until we meet again.

This is I, Achillion once more. As has been said, Magnus has already spoken to me, and informed me that you were in his area. It is interesting for you to meet up with other Devas and we can all work together towards helping man to help his and our planet to improve it, and make it a place of beauty once more. We of the higher realms, who work between the two worlds with nature, and hopefully with mankind, hope that this liaison can expand and become widespread, so that mankind will learn how to be a guardian of the Earth, and how to restore the balance of nature, and we hope that we can help in this respect, bringing about a change of heart and conditions. In future times, people will be more aware of their spirituality, and those who are being born into the world at this time are more fully integrated within their spirituality, and as they become adults they will help all the more, so that the whole world will be encompassed by a generation who care for the planet, and for nature. All the kingdoms of the planet will unite, and we the Devas hope that this will not take too long, so that there will not be irrevocable damage to all man's surroundings.

There has been so much change within your lifetime since you were small, change that has not been for the better in many ways regarding nature. There have always been floods and droughts, but it is becoming more prevalent, and mainly through mankind's treatment of the planet. You, we know would not endanger living creatures, and hope that the changes that will be brought about will begin soon. I, Achillion this day declare that the Devic Kingdom will work with man to the best of their ability, and it is hoped that the governments of the world will unite, and perhaps together with like-minded individuals to yourself, there can be a communication between the two worlds, so that help can be given to the planet. My blessing to you all this day. Achillion.

COMMUNICATIONS FROM THE DEVIC KINGDOM 2
MELODION, OAKWOOD WOODS-10

Melodion here, we saw you both coming in this direction and were pleased to greet you, there was a brightness around you that showed you were spiritually aware of us and could attune to us. It is very seldom that humans are able to hear our thoughts, and over the centuries here, very few have, so you are welcome. I know you communicate with Achillion, who is the Deva of the woods you visit at Swallowship and beyond. My domain is on the north side of the river and covers these woods near Oakwood and beyond.

There are many who would appreciate walking these woodland ways, you are fortunate to be aware of them, and also to be fit enough to traverse this way. You must make the most of the time you have left in your life to enjoy these beautiful areas that have been created for man to enjoy. Many do not know of such places, or are unable physically to come here, as you can only travel here by foot.

I know from your minds that you wish to be in unity and harmony with all living things, plant, tree, animal and insect. You have had a change of outlook since you have become spiritually aware, and now know all are one. All have a right to live just as much as man, which a number of people seem not to appreciate, participating as they do in the 'sport' of killing birds and animals needlessly and unnecessarily. There are also many who kill insects, particularly merely because they annoy them and mainly due to ignorance. Sometimes it is through fear of some insect that I know from your thoughts that you have had all your life, an unreasoning fear that you are attempting to conquer. However, now you have the insect removed instead of being killed because of your fear, which is an improvement.

Devas are beings who are described in a book you have at home as Landscape Angels, who overlight a large area, and have smaller individual Devas working with them. Devas who are in charge of each planet, bush or tree.

I will stop for a while because I think perhaps one may wish to speak to you.

Bracken Deva – I am delighted to be able to communicate with you, and get a feeling of lightness from you and a desire to help nature, man and God. My task is to help to beautify this area with the bracken unfolding, making it as perfect as I can. My very essence is within the fronds you touch. Melodion speaking, – Go with God, and in peace, please come back again.

73

COMMUNICATIONS FROM THE DEVIC KINGDOM 2
MELODION, OAKWOOD WOODS-11

This is Melodion and I welcome you back to our haven of peace and tranquillity, and is what you search for in your dwelling place. It will not be long before you find it, I promise you. Meanwhile, it is cool here, so it would be advisable to put on your extra layer of clothing. We are sorry that Gordon is indisposed, and we know that partly it is due to his longing to be free, but have faith it will not be long now. You know it is on its way, and why he is finding it harder to fight the flu that persists. As I was saying, your destiny is to work for God, and He has this plan for you that will come about this year, and your business will sell very quickly now, so hold on and your path will be a straight and true one towards that place for which you search.

Looking back on the time since first I spoke to you, much has occurred, and I realise you cannot really take it in, all the happenings, speaking with all the Devas, and communion with Higher Beings, particularly the Masters. There are many who would wish for this communication between themselves and Higher Beings, so you are greatly blessed, because it was something not looked for by you, but it was meant to be. You always felt there was something more than just a communication between yourself and those newly departed, although you felt it was an honour to be able to hear their thoughts and pass them on to others who needed them, you still felt there was something higher that you could not imagine, and yet you felt you had to be of service with this gift. Now you know the reason and what it was. Little did you imagine who you would be serving and in what way. Your life has changed and will never be the same again, but would you wish it to be so? I think not.

It is so pleasant to be able to communicate with one whose mind accepts each thought as it comes, and communicates through the voice. I too am blessed in being able to speak to you, and to tell you that all the Devic Kingdom hope and pray that mankind will turn towards us, and that we may serve you and God. God directs us, and we always serve Him, but we wish to help the Earth at this time in order to erase the pollution, and to turn aside all who would desecrate nature in its many forms. There are many ways of doing this, not always through man's ways, but we find ways of stopping this. Yes, you wondered where the sun had disappeared; it is because you are in the confines of the wood, but it is shining up the hill. Make your way there and be in the warmth of the sun again. Yes it seems more like autumn or spring than winter, and is the third week in January, when usually frost or snow is covering the ground, and icy winds. Today is a day of beauty, sunshine and blue skies, and warm in the sun. There is still winter to come, but obviously it will not last as long, starting off so well, so you are fortunate this year.

There is much to look forward to besides the weather. As the Master Jesus told you, today your new life is just beginning. You have

74

been marking time until the business is sold, and then you will move on and begin in earnest with your new Light Centre. We, and those who have spoken with you many times, hope to serve you and those Devas who will be within your garden, all of us hope to help you and others of like mind, to help mankind in whatever way we can. We know that part of your destiny is the teachings from the Masters; part of it is forming a Light Centre in this area, so that people from the north may join you in meditation, discussion, prayer and teaching. There will be many in the future who will look for this, who need this to straighten their footsteps along the way. Perhaps they have realised there is something more to life, but could not quite recognise what it was, as you did until the Teachings began, and until The Light Of The World spoke to you several times. He it is who overlights you all and He will guide you, both you and others who you will help.

In future days there will be meetings at your house, and you will help to point people in the right direction, to guide them through visualisation, which will prove a powerful influence throughout the world because Light Centres are desperately needed to uplift the consciousness of mankind, and also to provide a vision for the future, helping to illumine the mind and point man's service towards illumination of the soul, and towards improvements in conditions upon the Earth.

This wood has changed since you were here last. There has been a swathe cut through the trees that is sad, but there has been replanting, and those new young trees are protected by stakes and a covering, which seems to be increasing throughout the country. It is plastic I know, but tubing of some kind to protect the young tiny trees that will take the place of those that were cut down. This is all very well, but so many forests are being insidiously cut down at a tremendous rate, not particularly here, but in countries south of the equator, and as you know, replanting does not take place there, as people use the land for other purposes and this is causing a great silting up of river beds. The estuaries are completely altered; the course of the rivers changed, and therefore those in authority who understand what is being done must give educate these people. They need not push their way into the lives of those who don't understand, but merely explain the reason why this should not be done, and give them different land, so the forests are preserved for all time. Those forests have been in existence from time immemorial, and are necessary to balance nature and the climate.

The climate has changed throughout the globe, with this flooding and drought, but this balance must be regained, and it will be if man will realise what is happening by cutting down these forests and altering the land. The soil erodes as a result of the cut trees, and this causes a change in the area, and this change, if multiplied throughout the globe has to be redressed. It is part of our work as Devas, to try and put right what has been done, famine, drought and flood. We hope that man will help us in our task, and understand what it is that he must do. Your part of the world is less at risk, but the Armenian earthquake, although it was tragic as so many lost their lives, or had difficulty put into their lives as a result. It has brought about a closeness between the two hemispheres, the East and West, which has not occurred for centuries, so some good has come out of the tragedy.

There are little people in this wood who also wish to speak to you. Up until now I don't think they have spoken, so I will pass them on to you for a few minutes talk. "Thank you." We are here with you, we have watched you many times when you have come here and attuned to Melodion, and we have wanted to talk but you have been so busy just the two of you that you have not been aware of us, but we are very happy that you can commune with us for a few minutes now, and we hope that in the future you will hear us. This is wonderful, I have not spoken to a human for so long, and you are dressed in the colours we like, bright red, green, and white as well, lovely to us. "Could I ask who is speaking?" Yes, this is Tricia. It is rather like the name Patricia, but just the second half. I dress in similar colours to you, I love greens, nice bright colours, and I know that is one of your favourite colours at present, not the green of the woods necessarily, but slightly brighter, and I like turquoise as you do. These colours are healing and good for you. The colours you wear often represent the mood you are in. I do not know whether you have thought of this, but it is so, except for people who wear the same colour all the time! They must be in the same mood all the time mustn't they? I know your daughter Heather loves purple and that is the colour of royalty as you know, but it is also a healing colour. It is the colour of periwinkle, hyacinth and all manner of other wild flowers.

I do not wish to speak of colour all the time. My friends with me wish to welcome you and hope that you will speak with us again. We are gathered all around you although you cannot see us. Would you like to one day? I think you would. "Yes, I certainly would." Perhaps we will show ourselves to you when we have spoken to you a few times. How many do you think there are of us with you, the little people? "Well, perhaps about ten?" Oh no! There are lots more than ten here. There is a great band of us walking beside you and flying in the air. You cannot imagine how many. There must be nearly forty of us I think. "Oh that is wonderful!" Yes, I thought you would be pleased, because you always think that perhaps there will be one or two of us, but now you realise how fortunate you are and that there is a band of us who follow you around. You are never alone. I know that you realise that Melodion is here, but we too are always here. We will say farewell for now, and look forward to the next time, goodbye.

This is Melodion again. Yes, you had not imagined that there could be so many little people all around you and wanting to speak to you. I knew that you would be delighted when you discovered that they were there, and so many of them. I will let you move faster now because I think that you are getting rather cool, and I do not wish you to get Gordon's cold! My greetings to you all, you and those who are in your group. My

blessings be upon you this day. The next time you come, you will feel differently I know, because a step will have been taken in the right direction. God bless.
Melodion.

COMMUNICATIONS FROM THE DEVIC KINGDOM 2
MAGNON, HARESHAW LINN-12

Some time ago you visited our abode, and we are pleased to welcome your return and this time you are able to record what we say to you. Sadly, the day is not as warm as it might have been, certainly not as warm as it was when you left your house, but we hope that you will still enjoy your visit in our beautiful surroundings. The birdsong shows you that they are happy here, as we are, and the fast flowing waters coming over the fall is quite powerful. So far you have not asked the name of the one who speaks to you, I am the Deva of this area, and if you wish to know who it is I will tell you. Names are not really of great importance to us as you know, but if you really wish to know I will tell you. It is rather similar to the name of the Deva who spoke to you in the Kielder Forest; it is Magnon, and the one who spoke to you there was Magnus.

I have been overlighting this area for many centuries, and will continue to do so until my time limit is finished. It is one of these things that may seem strange to you, but when our time is up, we move on to other service. Not necessarily overlighting an area, but to do a different task to serve God, and therefore like yourselves, through incarnations you learn a little more each time. In this service we too learn in different ways by taking a variety of tasks, we learn how it is to serve in a different manner, sometimes it is serving nature, and at other times it is purely service for God. This is a place of beautiful surroundings, particularly when the weather is warm and the trees are leafy. At present you can see right across to the other side, whereas in the summer very little can be viewed through the leaves. The little people here have been very busy, and the nature spirits have been working very hard as the winter has been reasonably mild, and although you saw snow here on your journey, it has not been as thick as usual. I will allow you to continue with your walk because I think that you are feeling rather cold and I will speak to you further along. Farewell for now.

We, the little people also wish to welcome you to our abode. We spoke to you before, and it was us who spoke, not the Deva of the place. It is so nice to be able to have someone who can hear our thoughts, and record them as well. Welcome back, and we hope that you will come back many times from time to time throughout your lives, because this is a beautiful place, and we are very happy here with the rushing waters and trees. We have been in a state of activity throughout the winter, because that is a time when we help nature to work its small miracle each year, bringing forth new buds, and keeping the sap in the trees moving. It is part of our work to help, and we are happy to be in this area of beauty. We know that this day to you is cold, and we sense your chilliness. We do not wish to keep you if you wish to move on, but all the same, we still wished to talk to you before you got nearer to the waterfall, where our voices would be drowned out, literally. Farewell for now. "Who is speaking?" I am Langrost, and I am an elf, and it is my pleasant duty to be the spokesman. Farewell.

There is quite a family of wild life in this area. Many things that you cannot see are small creatures and birds who dwell in this sort of environment, which they prefer as it is near water, and with protection of the rocks, trees and undergrowth. It really is beautiful with the rushing waters, and yet the calm beyond. I feel that it is a perfect area as far as I am concerned, particularly on beautiful summer days, when the sky and water are both blue. You have been here on a day when it was warm, so you can remember how inviting the water looked, although I know you would not wish to plunge down the waterfall! The water in the river or beck can be a place where many people have cooled their hot limbs in warmer weather. Remember that everywhere has its own beauty, which is in the eye of the beholder, and if you look at any place on this Earth, you can find beauty and God's hand behind it.

Just a few last words to wish you well on your continuing work. We know you have begun to work for God, and He will protect and guide you, and He will help you in any way possible. Just trust, believe, and know that your steps are being guided along the true path. He will secure everything that is necessary for the future, I know that you are aware of what I mean. Be strong in the Lord, and know that He protects all His children. Your work is to continue for the rest of your lives, this we know, and there will be many who will speak through you and I'm happy to be one, and if I can help in any way I will be very pleased to do so. Every reassurance periodically helps, and I think you have felt a little comfort today in what has been said both from me, and those who spoke in your meditation. God be with you and protect you all.

We are here again just to say goodbye, and we hope next time you come it will be a lovely warm day, and you will be completely on your own without interruptions, although those who were present did not disturb you at all, and we hope that the peace in this place will seep into you, and you will remember it for some time to come, even though it was rather cold. So we will say goodbye and God bless. This is Langrost speaking again. "Goodbye."
Magnon and Langrost.

CHANNELLED COMMUNICATIONS FROM THE DEVIC KINGDOM

Book Three

BERYL CHARNLEY

CHANNELLED COMMUNICATIONS FROM THE DEVIC KINGDOM
Book Three

CONTENTS

Channelled by Beryl Charnley

COMMUNICATIONS FROM THE DEVIC KINGDOM 3
ACHILLION AND FRIENDS, SWALLOWSHIP WOODS-1

I am the spirit of the tree, and as sentinels of this forest, we have hoped that you would commune with us, as you commune with the Deva of the forest and the countryside beyond, and with the little people who live here. We two sentinels have stood here since ages past. Many have come and gone over the years, but few have been able to hear our voice; indeed you are the first to record our thoughts. From time immemorial it seems, we have grown and gradually looked over the surrounding area, now in splendour, but sadly much has been cut down around us. This does occur from time to time, and must do to make way for new trees. The saplings you see which are starting to spread and have room to breathe and grow, nevertheless, our companions of the past have been destroyed, but we stand with others of our kind, and will do for a long time to come.

We know that humanity is becoming more aware of the possibility of danger to the environment. This danger is being intensified, as has been proved by the destruction of much of the rain forest areas in warm parts of the world, and of course, the area surrounding the planet is being affected by much of man's technological advancement, but in a different way. Although man has advanced materially, he has not been advancing spiritually, and only when certain members of humanity over the last few decades have slowly become aware; trying to improve their capabilities, and realised that they can hear our thoughts. We, the tree spirits enjoin with the Devas and the little people in appealing to you to help in whatever way you can to improve the conditions for nature in all its forms. Plants, trees, wildlife, do what you can in your own way to help us, and I know you will. We feel responsible for our forest, and in our responsibility we represent forests throughout the globe, so remember that we depend on you and others of like mind throughout the Earth. We appeal to you and hope you will appeal to others who have more responsibility than you have. We hope you will return and perhaps things will have improved by the next visit. We are happy to greet you and know that you have an affinity for nature, so you go with our blessing and hope for the future...

...Achillion here, welcome to you all. As you see, your place of peace, tranquillity and beauty is being despoiled, but you must look ahead to the time to come when the small trees that will be planted, and those which have already began to grow will take over in this area that has been cleared. It is sad to see, and I know that you felt quite strongly as you passed it, that foreigners had invaded the area. Someone with a transistor radio who takes away the dead logs, and thinks nothing of the beauty surrounding him. This is humanity today, but we hope that humanity will have a different attitude, similar to your own. You may have noticed that the bird song seems to have become louder in this forest, and it is partly due to the clearing. They do not normally sing in areas that are too enclosed, and therefore in some ways it has been a benefit for the birds. There is always a benefit for something when there is change, but because you have been so used to beautiful woods surrounding you, have always thought how lovely that everything was as it has been, for the years you have known it. However, change becomes evident everywhere, and this is something that occurs throughout life, change for the better or worse, but a change should be made, or else things will eventually get in a rut, and this should not be.

There should always be change for the better, to benefits the surroundings, and you will find that in a few years time, if you return here, that there will be new saplings that have been planted, and will be doing well in the open, which could not have happened, had the woods remained as they were. Therefore, nature and man must change before the world becomes as it should and will be, better in every way.

I think the insect life is becoming rather bewildered by this mild weather, as you have noticed. There are the small spiders, and also midgies are flying about, which does not normally occur until much later. This winter has been extremely mild and it shows that the seasons are changing very perceptibly, and this part of the country in the future will be quite warm when the changes occur. They have been changing and so the climate has altered. It is not always a sudden change, but in time to come there may be a more dramatic change, and this will have to occur before mankind takes note.

So many people blindly follow the ways they have always done, heeding nothing but their own enjoyment, but thought must be given for man's surroundings, and if there are more of you that will do this, then the changes will be less dramatic. In the early days of climate change there were insufficient people who had thought for the morrow, and the planet Earth, and therefore the changes might be sweeping if this is still the case. Sweeping aside those who are heedless and thoughtless for the planet and the continuation of all species of life. However, today is a day of beauty, and you are out to enjoy yourselves, and I do not wish to speak of doom and gloom, but of better things to come for all of you. This will be, so have faith and know the prophecies will come to pass. You have had a long wait, but it will not be long now, I promise you.

You ask about the changes, and know now that the Earth is a living entity, and is capable of reacting to over-pollution and over-erosion. This is something that you have learnt over the last few years, and it must be realised that God who created the Earth, all the other planets and everything that is, knew that this could occur. Because in creating living planets, He knew that the planet itself would shrug off anything that was irritating and destroying the delicate balance of nature and all that lives upon the Earth, and man through his overpopulation as well as his over-pollution and destruction has caused irrevocable changes. In time the Earth through God will have to bring about changes that will restore the Earth to full health, vigour, and balance similar to the way that an animal or man would bring about a change if something were causing an irritation or annoyance. So God knew that this would occur if man continued in the way that he was doing at present, and unless man makes great changes within his living conditions, these changes must occur, so that the Earth can be restored and continue in its normal existence. I think perhaps this is all I can say on the matter.

Do not worry unduly about the changes, because as I or your guides have said, that you will be protected, and also all who are aware of what is happening and are spiritually aware, they will be given protection and warning if there is any danger likely to occur in their areas, and should there be the need for transportation by vehicles from other planets, you will be. This is something that has been foretold for many years, but be of good cheer and know that all will be well with you and yours.

Yes, when the changes occur it will be a time for a moving upwards into a higher dimension, a higher state of being, and this is God inspired. The Earth herself could not do this of her own accord, but it will be something that would occur at one and the same time, and even if you were transported from the Earth on a spacecraft, you would then be taken into the fourth dimension at the same time. If you were still upon the Earth, this would still occur, but perhaps in a less dramatic way. It is something that is difficult to describe to you as you cannot imagine another dimension apart from what you have been told about, becoming more amorphous and aware of other beings and worlds that you cannot see at present. Everything will come in due course, but that part of the change has been and will be ordained by GOD and his servants. You were suggesting that originally those who lived on Lemuria and Atlantis had been four dimensional, but the Earth herself has always been upon the third dimension. Those who came to live upon it in those days were less physical in their bodies, but this was purely because they had come from other planets, and gradually they became more material through living on the third dimension, so there has never been a state of the fourth dimension upon the Earth until now. This is for the future.

...Yes, we are here, and this time it is Tatum who speaks. Janus allowed me to take his place today for a momentary talk, because I know that your tape is running low, and we just wish to have our little say to let you know that we have been accompanying you all the way through the woods. We saw you with the tree at the beginning, and then we followed you until now, but we have kept very quiet, allowing you to have your say, and Achillion who overlights us all was in charge, of course. We just wanted you to know that we always accompany you on your expeditions, and are happy to greet you each time. As you can see, we have been very busy as the little people were where you visited two days ago. You see we know everything that you do, word gets around quite fast! We are in hiding, and it is very seldom that we show ourselves, but perhaps one day, as we said before you will see us, just a glimpse! So, we will say

84

farewell because we know that you will wish to have words with Achillion. Farewell for now...

...Those stories, the myths of Greek and Roman times, have come about as a result of real beings, and legend throughout the world speaks of these people who have done deeds of great prowess. They were indeed beings who were capable of much more than mere man was able to do. As a result, they were revered by humanity, and they were from space as you call it, from other planets, evolved beings who helped humanity to overcome evil in past times, and as a result, these legends have grown. Even in the Bible it was said in those times there were giants, and traces of giants have been found throughout the world. They too were a race apart, not necessarily from other planets, but a race that was called the Titans. There have been many root races of men, and this was one that failed to survive, rather like the dinosaurs. Legend deals with many things, but that is another story, so perhaps another time we can deal in more depth, regarding the myths and legends from the past. I think we have covered many different topics today, and it has been interesting to discuss things with you that you queried. I give you my blessing and look forward to our next meeting.

ACHILLION AND FRIENDS, SWALLOWSHIP WOODS-3
TINA-2

When you walk amongst woodland areas, and by streams and lakes, there is always someone with you, you may not see us, but know that the Deva of that area is watching over you. I, Tina, am here with you now and am happy to greet you, all of you this lovely morning. All of nature is just at the point of waking, as you have seen by the lake, and all that is alive is becoming more vital. The nature spirits have been helping, it has been such a mild winter that everything is way ahead of normal, so there is much to see today on your visit.

What your daughter, Heather, saw last time you visited here after I had spoken was symbolic of what I was giving, I was giving energies to the nature spirits who were attending to the needs of the vegetation in this woodland area. The energies that I receive from above are given freely when necessary, for all growing things. At certain times of the year it is more essential for energies to be directed towards the trees and undergrowth. This is a time when they particularly need this help, and which may have been receiving help over the last month or two, for it is a time of growth. Once established through the winter, all growing things need help to survive and become whole. I look after this area of the landscape for several miles around, and have been doing so for many ages. (I realise that from time to time you must stop to allow people to pass who would not understand what you are doing. Perhaps they may think you are getting inspiration for a book!).

Q. I would like to know about something I have seen recently during meditations, it is like a centrifugal force of energy that turns either clockwise or anticlockwise, in the ether. I have also seen structures in connection with it like a pentagon-dodecahedron, and other structures surrounding this, I would just like to know more about it.

A. The patterns and structures you have seen are energies within the atmosphere. Some people can see these, as you can, and many live their lives through being completely unaware of them. They are often seen in the atmosphere within the countryside, in mountainous areas and beside lakes and streams. They are all to do with the energies that you saw, supposedly my hands giving out energies. I do not have hands, but the symbol was there, and these energies that you have seen are similar to the glowing ball of light that you saw here the last time. I think that was what you saw. It is a different form of energy being given in a general pattern to all living things. It is a wider scope of energy rather than a concentrated form, and that is the only way I can describe it. At times you may see energies coming from the sun, which is a great source of light and energy to all growing things. I know that you cannot look up to the sun, but you can see the energies streaming down from it at times if you look in the general direction. It is difficult to describe how these forms take shape. They vary in structure, but those that you have seen have been given to the surrounding landscape for use by the various life forms.

Looking at the trees around you, you can see the stark fingers of the twigs and branches at present, with very little sign of life, but looking closer you can see that even the beech has its buds ready with leaves coiled up within them, so that the life forces is shown to be running through the veins of the tree right to the furthermost tips. Although they look bare, there is life waiting to burst forth in all its glory, as the spring flowers have already done, so they will do soon.

Devas are usually reckoned to be sexless, but there are a few like myself who have female names, though in the main there is little to tell of any difference between male and female, it is purely in the name and perhaps the feeling that you may get from my presence. There may be a slight difference from that of your friends Achillion, Melodion, or others who you have met on your journeys. I do not think there is anything more that I wish to tell you this morning. It has been pleasant to communicate with you, and we have been fortunate that there have been few people around to disturb us. I will be happy to communicate whenever I see you again, and perhaps you may have more questions to ask. In the meantime, my blessing be upon you all, and I hope you enjoy your day. God bless.

COMMUNICATIONS FROM THE DEVIC KINGDOM 3
MELODION-3

My greetings to you all, I have been watching you coming ever nearer, and hoping that this day we might meet. We have not met for some time, and I am very happy to speak to you once more. The last time Beryl came on her own on a warm day in the winter, and it was nice to have communication. Now, as you see life is sprouting in the trees, and everything is becoming new again in the springtime of the year. Renewal of all kinds, and we hope a new beginning for you. It is certain that there will be a sale and your work will begin in earnest this year, when your centre is born. That centre is to be a very important feature in the North of England. You are already thinking of ways in which to broach the subject to others in the form of a booklet, which in itself would make things more straightforward to you. If it is straightened out in your minds, then you can apply these thoughts to other people. As you say, collating the information into a more concise booklet, bringing to bear all the facts that you have learnt over the last few years, and attempting to put them into a form of communication of how life has come about. From its very beginnings, from God to the universes, trying to bring it into everyday life as it is at present. It is a difficult task, but a rewarding one that will bring forth other ideas.

As our Lord, the Master Jesus said to you today, the time has come to spread your net a little wider to others who we hope will be interested in what you have to tell them. Others who may have a little knowledge, that with the help of your booklet, may begin to make sense of the whole, and set their minds wondering, so that they will come back for more information in the future. Not necessarily directly, it may take them a while, but this seed thought will have been put in their minds, and in time to come they will return. You will find that as time progresses, you will be guided as to how to approach people, and help them in the ways that they need help. Each one different from the other, and thinking in a different way, certainly not always in the same way you do, nevertheless, there will be many that you approach who you may have doubts about. Quite often though, you will find that in some way their thoughts are very similar to your own, rather similar to some of the teachings you have been given, and you might be pleasantly surprised at their reaction. Always be ready to be rebuffed, as others have been in the past, but you must continue regardless, having started this work, and I know you are extremely keen and earnest to continue, and now that you have thoughts of the book, you will be enthusiastic about starting it.

Yes, here you see the two sides of man's nature; one is the physical, destructive side, with spent cartridges lying, and the other is the creative, beautiful side, where he has planted bulbs for generations to come, so that flowers will bloom in memory over the years, and spread in abundance to make a place of peace and tranquillity. So they are a sign of hope, and we will look upon that as being fair, fair to man's nature, because there is only a minority who are destructive. There are many who are thoughtless, who do not realise what they are doing, but if they have the faults pointed out to them, where they are failing, they will understand and put them right, most of them anyway. Therefore we have hope for man in the future, that he will improve the conditions around him.

Yes Beryl, you think to yourself, I speak his words but I don't know what he looks like, so perhaps I should describe myself for you. I am a Being of Light with energies sprouting from where my shoulders might be. I am a Being roughly twice your height, if not three times, and in the past those who have been able to see a little of what we look like, have shown us with wings. It is because of the energies shooting upwards and outwards from us that give that appearance of light and softness. My colours are quite bright, of yellows, silver and a soft blue. I say they are quite bright because they are so compared with colours that you think of, of an iridescent light. There is orange there too, so it is rather fiery in aspect, so in the future, perhaps you can picture me in a better way.

Yes, so it is that the old makes way for the new in forests from time to time, the trimming back must be done to give new growth a chance to expand. It is sad to see the trees cut down, but this must be done, good husbandry, and in time to come the new ones will be tall and straight. If others were not cut and trimmed, they could not stand straight and grow to their full height, so that this must occur, sad as it is. You see a little tree in front of you, that has had to move to get light, and as a result is twisted, therefore, it is necessary to produce tall straight trees, and the songs of birds ring out in this new clearing…

…At last we have our opportunity to speak to you, and we are very happy to do so. We have followed you all the way through the woods and there are many of us here. You would not believe we are all around you, on the ground and in the air, sitting on your shoulders if you could see us, but we are so happy to see you and to find someone who is aware of us. We have only spoken once before, and that was when you were here on your own, Beryl, but we hope that each time now we will be allowed a few moments to be in touch with you. When you came to draw these trees, Heather, we were clustered all around you, and we were those who beckoned to you today to suggest you came along this path. You tried once to find this part of the woods, and thought it was lost forever, but now you know it is still here, and the same as when you originally saw it. We are always with these trees because they are so old, and we have lived here within and around them for a long time. The one who has been speaking to you is Jarus, similar to Janus, but with a different letter. A lot of our names are rather similar to one another. You have our blessing this day, and perhaps next time we can speak a little longer. Farewell for now…

…Now I return. You know there is much work ahead of you, many types of work besides the centre, and the books you will produce. There is also the work that you have promised to do in blessing and revitalising certain areas that need this work done. Therefore, your footsteps are leading you along a new path in your lives, and I know that you are eager to begin. You have been led on this path because you chose to do this work in this incarnation, this worthwhile work that you have barely begun. The teachings that you will be given, and have been given, will help you, but you must do the work, the deeds coming from the thoughts and the word. So, I wish you well in your new life, and I hope that by the next time you come here you will have signed and sealed the pact for the business to end and your new life to begin. God bless you all.

COMMUNICATIONS FROM THE DEVIC KINGDOM 3
MELODION-4

I, Melodion, greet you on this beautiful morning. I know that you have come for other purposes besides my communication, but I am pleased to welcome you on behalf of Warden Hill. It is a sacred site, and will benefit from your administrations and invocation for the blessing of God upon it. I think that you, Heather, have a question to ask me.

Q. Yes, I was just thinking as it is called a fort on the top of that hill, as on many other hills, whether it has been used for warlike purposes, or was the fort more of a fortification for a dwelling of a sacred kind?

A. Yes, that is a good question. It has been used for a variety of purposes in the past, mainly as a protective measure for dwellings. For some reason all are called forts, but I suppose this covers a variety of reasons for a hollowed-out site on the top of a hill. It was used occasionally for warlike purposes, but in the main they were dwellings, and there was a sacred area where votive offerings were given for mainly worship of the sun, and for this reason it was made on a hill, to be as near the sun as possible.

Q. Could you tell me the person who rules over the moon, as Apollo is to the sun? I would be interested to know the name of the being who rules the moon.

A. The only name I am aware of is Luna. In the main we do not deal with names. It is always a matter of consideration when we are asked our names, because we are all part of that great consciousness that comes from the Source of all beings, but Luna is the only name that springs to mind regarding the moon.

Yes, you are attempting to visualise what I look like, hoping that this will help you to come closer. It is difficult to describe oneself, but I am basically a column of light, with colours exuding around me, particularly at the top, so that it appears flame-like, not like the rays of the sun, more like large flame shaped moving patterns of light. Think of me as being a silvery white light, surrounded by flames of blue, turquoise and gold. They are the colours that in the main surround me. The colours are mainly iridescent, so therefore they are not exactly as you were picturing them, more metallic and shining, should we say. It is difficult to describe something that is not material or physical, but unearthly. You are surprised with the warmth in the sun, pleasantly of course. Now we have a tractor coming towards us, so perhaps I had better stop, but always be ready for my word, sometimes it comes unexpectedly!

Q. I know you wish to ask a question regarding whether there is a Head Deva for each country?

A. This is a moot point, because in the main the Archangel Michael is overlighting the Earth at this time, and He is above us all. We have orders directly from the Archangels and Masters of the Hierarchy, and as a result there is no need for separate Devas for each country. All of us are aware of the areas in which we work, and those areas that we overlight, spread for quite a number of miles. Therefore, there is no need to have one who is above each one of us in the country. I hope that answers your question. "Yes, thank you." The individual small devas in charge of plant life, and those who nurture the trees are all overlit by us, the Landscape Angels, this term has been used at Findhorn. It is a good name, because we cover a large area, and therefore I, for instance, overlight the landscape surrounding here. So the small devas work on their own in charge of their particular plants.

Q. I keep seeing this image like a disk of light, or at the least, a whole skyful of light. I think the trees take their energy from it. Is this a spiritual layer from the actual spiritual realms?

A. Yes, you are seeing energy that is being given out from the Higher Realms, from ourselves for the devas of all kinds to absorb, and use for all life forms, the trees in particular. This is something that not many see, and this is a great thing to be able to see such energy forms. Sometimes it is in the form of a flat plane of light, and sometimes a ball of light that is smaller. Have you seen anything resembling a ball of light?

The only thing I saw was at Wallington, and I thought that one of the devas there was holding a small ball of light in his hands, and was distributing it to the other beings there. Is that what you mean?

Yes, that is really the main conception of the Essence of life, which is given to each group of small devas, who take the life force, that energy to renew the life force within all growing things, this is given to them by ourselves. The hands that you may have seen may have been in your mind. It could have been the way in which it was conveyed to you, but we do not have hands as such, but the idea is absolutely correct. The Blessing of God the Father has been given to you this day and to the sacred site you have visited. God bless, Melodion.

COMMUNICATIONS FROM THE DEVIC KINGDOM 3
ACHILLION-5

My greetings to you both today. Each time you do your recording, you seem to be dogged by people, this time you thought you had the wood to yourselves, but it seems that there are forces about, there are little tents and hides all over the wood. Something that has not been present before, and shooting! However, we will do our best. It is nice to see you both, and I will accompany you through the wood. If I am not present on the photograph, perhaps someone else will be. Do you have questions to ask me?

Q. Would it be a help to us if we were to be told about a day in the life of a little person or a Deva?

A. It may possibly be helpful. It is rather difficult to judge whether it will be beneficial or not. I know that you wish to understand more about the little people, and the work concerned with devas, plants and trees. I think that we would have to arrange this in advance if you feel you would like to know more. I think that it could be a way of understanding. If we get together we can organise this for you, and attempt to let you know what is concerned in daily life with the devas. You are aware of course, of the energies that they use to instil life force into all growing things, and this is part of their daily life. We will consider this and let you know, because there will have to be some work done together before we can launch forth on a dissertation. I think you will understand this.

Q. How can we help Devas to help the Earth at this time?

A. We of the Devic Kingdom would consider it an honour to communicate and work with you in order to help the Earth. We know that you have great hopes that we can work together, and I am sure that this will be part of the Plan, part of your work for the future, communicating with us and finding out more details. We feel that if you and others like you can form a body to approach your local member of Parliament, and broach certain questions to him, suggesting various methods to avoid pollution and local trouble throughout the United Kingdom, then this is a beginning. There are far-reaching necessities of course, including the rain forests that are being daily swept aside, and pollution of the seas, but if you were to get together with other like-minded individuals and attempt to work out a plan of campaign, then in the future we can try to resolve any difficulties by combining forces. Those devas with whom you are in contact, Melodion and myself, and any others who may be able to help, we too will try to work out some kind of plan for you.

Q. Do you, Achillion, think that we are ready to help at this point in time?

A. Yes, I would say you are now. Perhaps a few months back was not the time, but I think now you have become accustomed to this method of communication and you have the instruments to record and print our words, so you can now send out our communications to others of like mind. There will be many in the North of England and in other parts of the country who would be interested in helping, I am sure. If communication was made between you, then others who are, perhaps, in attunement with the devas in their part of the country might also help. The idea is a very good one, of networking communication between mankind and the Devic Kingdom, to give all help possible.

Q. Is it intended that we start this work before going to the Light Centre?

A. Certainly it is, you have already begun. There is nothing to stop you from doing this work wherever you are. Obviously, you will have more time once you have your Light Centre, and the business is sold, but there is nothing to stop you at any time working with us, and working for the good of nature and the Planet.

Q. Landscape temples and ley lines are of great importance, I feel. How can we make best use of them, by sending out light, or water and stone ceremonies, or is there more we can do?

A. This is quite a large question involving several things. Certainly by sprinkling water from the holy wells, and arranging stones from those areas in sacred places is a great benefit to the area, and ley lines quite often lead from these places and spread their lines across the country. Of course, ley lines are beneficial, particularly if your property is on one, there is an upliftment within that house. Ley lines can be used in different ways, they are a linking between sacred sites or hills and churches, and I think that there could be a help in knowing where they run. This would have to be considered, it is not absolutely essential. It is the sacred sites and the Earth herself, and growing things that are of more importance than ley lines and landscape temples. They are important, but they complicate things a little, and it is not essential to know about these for the work you are doing.

Q. I would be interested in advice on dealing with negative sites.

A. Yes, you spoke of a particular negative site last night with your co-workers, and this is a place that needs upliftment. It is worth considering before you go, what prayers you will use and how you will traverse the site. It is as well if it is a church, to begin at the entrance with a prayer using the holy water and stones. Walk around the church with this water, sprinkling on each corner, saying the Lord's Prayer as you go, and say 'in the name of the Father, and of the Son and of the Holy Ghost', and as you go you could put a cross on each corner. This would be the same wherever you went, if it is a church or house or just an area. Once inside, you must stand at the back of the church and say the Lord's Prayer, invoking God's blessing upon that holy house. Then the sign of the cross could be made on the floor of the church with the holy water. Moving forward as you go towards the chancel, you do not need to say the prayers aloud, but the more of you there, the better, because this will give extra energy and upliftment. Think positively and lift up your hearts and minds, never allow that negativity to touch you. When you reach the chancel steps, say the Great Invocation, and then when you reach the altar, the Lord's Prayer can be said, and I think that then it will have made a great difference to the vibrations of that church, house or place you have visited. I hope this answers your question.

'Yes, thank you very much Achillion.'

There is not much tape left, but it has been nice to be with you, and answer your questions. I am always here whenever you need me, and if the weather is not to your liking, whether it is wet or very cold, then you can ask me to come to your house. I will come willingly, for I know where you live, and it is not far, so either Melodion or I can come to you if this is necessary.

'Thank you very much.'

I give you both my blessing this day, and hope that I have helped in some way in the work you have begun.

God bless, Achillion.

COMMUNICATIONS FROM THE DEVIC KINGDOM 3
ACHILLION-6

Yes, we are here! We thought we would surprise you by greeting you before Achillion came on the tape! We are very pleased to see you both on this very cold day. We did not think you would be able to manage to come because of the rain, but we will just say hello and goodbye, and will see you and speak to you later on, goodbye!

Greetings to you both, this is Achillion. I did not expect you to come either, because the weather is not conducive to turning out, but I think that you wish to contact us and have a little fresh air after being in most of the week. It is a shame when people are free, that the weather has changed so much after such beautiful days, however, you have braved the cold to speak to us, and we are pleased. Yes, what a shame that this driveway is all spoiled for the time being, with the wheel marks churning up the surface, but it will soon return to normal, and you are sad to see all the trees piled up ready to take away. This does happen periodically, and I think that this is the first time that you have come across it in this wood, but they have to make way for the replanting of the new, as I said before, and it will be put to good use. The trees accept this as part of their life, and those very tall, beautiful, straight ones will be used for telegraph poles and similar uses. They will not be chopped up just for firewood, so they will be serving a useful purpose.

I think you have a question at the back of your mind, Beryl, and it is one that was asked some time ago by Nicky regarding midgies and other insects that annoy and cause distress to humans, and how is it that they can be treated without doing them harm, so that they do not do this. This is a good question, and something that needs quite a bit of thought, because I know that she does not wish to kill them unless it is absolutely essential. You can spray yourself with an anti-mosquito spray or dab it on your wrists and forehead, so that it deters them to a large extent. It is not something that will kill them, but it will stop them from biting, keep them away, and in this way perhaps she could be saved from insect bites, but maybe she has tried this to no avail. The only alternative is to pray to them that they will go elsewhere, away from her and those who they are pestering, and if this fails, then the only alternative is, I am afraid, to spray the air, but this is something that we are very much against because most of these sprays as a rule affect the ozone layer. Some are approved, as you have discovered, and they are finding another propellant that doesn't affect the atmosphere, but I know that it will kill anything that will come into the path of the spray, and I know that this is something she does not wish to do. Apart from the other two alternatives, that is all that is left, I am afraid.

Achillion, could you tell us whether the climate will be affected when the changes come, and whether this part of the world will be warmer than at present?

96

I think that it is more than likely it will become a good deal warmer. As you have seen by the climate this winter, it is changing quite quickly even now, and the changes have barely begun. If they are to be gradual, then there will be a gradual warming up of this area of the world; it will become more of a temperate zone, as it was previously. When it was part of Hyperborea, it was quite a warm climate, and different trees and fruits grew in abundance. So I think it can be safely said that exotic fruits and vegetables could be grown even outside eventually, but certainly begun in greenhouses, so you might like to try keeping stones of avocados and any other pips or stones you might feel would be worth trying to grow. Start them off indoors, and then we hope you will have a greenhouse in the next property you buy. I know that is your plan, and all these things can be tried out within the greenhouse before the climate changes. I am certain that in the main it will be warmer most of the year, there would of course still be a winter, but not so severe as you have been used to in the past.

You were asking, Heather, which parts of the country would be most affected when the changes come. Certainly the south coast, because parts of that are already being eroded, and the Thames river has been having problems of recent years, and their flood prevention scheme will not prove to be effective when this time comes, unfortunately. Floods will overcome so many parts of the south, and parts of the east coast particularly below the North East, the Norfolk area, where it is very flat will be flooded. Other parts, it is difficult to say exactly where it will occur, but those two are the most obvious. Anyone who is spiritually aware will be protected, and guided to where it is known it will be safe when the time comes. Yes, many ancient monuments such as Stonehenge will be preserved, and Avebury, all these sacred places, the Dragon Hill at Uffington, of course, would be out of reach if there were a flood. It will not just be floods, for the Earth itself will move, and those places that are low shall be high, so there is no knowing at present how this will be affecting the British Isles. As I say it will be quite safe for you and those who you know can be warned. There will be many changes brought about, and you will have to be prepared for hardship for some time to come, so where you go to live will have to be a place of safety. You will be guided in this I know, so do not worry, all will be well for you and yours.

As you were saying, there were different ways of moving large stones, both by sound and ship. The use of sound helped many in the past to raise up enormous stones, but it had to be a combined sound, with large numbers of people employed for this, and as Heather said, she felt she had seen a picture of Stonehenge with water in the background. There were quite a number of changes in Britain in the past, and at many times water has been in places where it is miles distant now. There were means of transporting the stones from Wales that have not occurred to people. Historians have tried to work out how they managed to manoeuvre such monoliths, but I think you will find that one method was on the water, transported up in long barges to where it is now. Where it

97

has been for so many centuries, perhaps in the future it may be raised up on the top of a hill. Who knows? It will still be facing in the right direction, and unchanged in the use for which it was built, so long ago. It is difficult to say whether more stones will need replacing when the changes come. I think the best thing is to wait and see, because it may be many years ahead, and you would not be involved, Beryl, but I am sure that Heather will be, however, she will be kept informed of what will be necessary. It may be that there will be sites found that people do not know about at present, that were used in past days, but that is yet to come. I will say farewell for now, and allow your little friends to speak to you for a while. 'Thank you.'

Here we are! We have beaten you to it this time, and arrived in an unexpected place, you usually find us further down the track don't you? We thought we would surprise you today. That's twice now we have taken you by surprise! Your friend, Heather, was asking whether we are affected by pesticides. We of course are not, being on a different vibration to humans, but naturally small flowers, plants or vegetation are affected, because there is a cycle of life within all beings that affects everything. The balance of nature is altered if there is much spray used, and therefore tiny insects that you can barely see affect the cycle. If they are wiped out, then they affect the creatures that live on them, and therefore everything is affected, including the plant itself. So, we are affected and have to try to overcome this, but fortunately for us here, we have not found any difference, because no sprays are used in this vicinity. So, please remember this when you get your new garden, and try to avoid as far as possible, using sprays for insects and annoying pests. Try to use natural products where you can, when you get your kitchen garden, which I know you plan to do, using things that will foil the carrot fly and similar. Think up ways and means so that they will fly past instead of going straight for your carrots!

Is it not beautiful in this sunshine, it was worth coming after all, was it not? Yes it is lovely now, and quite sheltered here too, you found it cold and windy when you first got out of the car, but here we are sheltered, so always remember this. Come here on a windy day! There are many of us here, observing your progress through the wood. I know that you hardly believed how many were following you when you were with Melodion, but I would say there are nearly that number surrounding you now, which you would not have thought, would you? Who is it that speaks today? It is Janus who is usually the spokesman for everyone. Your friend Olivia is here as well, and she wishes to be remembered to you both. She is the one who has come nearest to showing herself to you, and anybody, and perhaps she will be the first to show herself to you in reality. I too might perhaps be persuaded to show myself to you. I know you do not like to be taunted. You know that we were only having fun. Yes, there are children playing down by the water, so perhaps it is just as well to stay here out of sight, and out of sound. We hope that in the future you will think of more things to ask us, some different questions about the work we do.

You see that we have buds on the trees already, which usually do not show themselves until much later, and many of the trees you passed as you came down are well ahead, as it has been such a mild winter. Maybe in the future it will be like this always. I know you hope so, so do we. When the snow comes, normally all the bulbs and small plants are covered, but they are kept warm from the cold winds. It is a kind of insulation for them, and they continue growing underneath, as you know, until they emerge as a pleasant surprise for you. These are the snowdrops and tips of crocus normally; instead they are in flower as now. The cold does not really serve any other purpose apart from giving life to growing things and bringing moisture to all the Earth, as the rain does. We will say farewell for now and allow Achillion to have the last few words, goodbye.

I, Achillion, say to you and your group, that you are greatly blessed by beings who are in communication with you, and who are guiding you on your path to form that centre of light. There are very few who have amongst their guides, two Masters of the Hierarchy, and Devas who are constantly in communication with you, also the little people from time to time. So think of yourselves as being very honoured by this and never take anything for granted which I know that you do not. Remember always to keep this in your mind for future times. I give you all my blessing this day, and wish you well for the future.
"Thank you."

God bless, Achillion.

COMMUNICATIONS FROM THE DEVIC KINGDOM 3
ACHILLION-7

I give you all my greetings in these different surroundings. It is pleasant to be able to speak to you in your own garden on such a beautiful day. I suggested coming to you instead of you coming to me, as all of you have much work to do in the garden to tidy it up after the wintertime, and after your various injuries, so that you were unable to cope earlier. It is nice to see you all enjoying the sunshine, and I am happy to greet you and to come here. With me it is but a second's thought, and then I am with you, whereas there is more involved when you come to meet me, walking, which Gordon finds difficult at times, and driving the car, and all of you making the effort, whereas this time it is only I who move from one situation to another. You have heard of teleportation I know, well that is not the way to think of it with myself, as I am already a Being of Light. I just project my light further. That is the only description I can give you, but perhaps in that you can understand the difference between moving a Being of Light, as opposed to a physical being. I believe that you have a question ready, which I will be happy to answer if I can.

Q. Well it is merely that we wondered if there is anything that we can do to help the Earth at this time, anything other than words. I know that we are attempting to send forth to others what you have said, but so far we have not covered many people. Is there anything further that we can do directly?

A. You are light bringers, come to illuminate mankind as well as yourselves, and you hope that in forming your permanent centre of light, you will be able to further extend your work, in bringing our thoughts to others. This in itself is an important part of your own work, but besides that, you could help people to understand the needs of the Earth at this present time. Many are learning much more this time period, people are increasingly aware of the Earth's predicament at this time. There has been much on television and in the papers regarding the rain forests and the climate. I know that you have been aware of this for some time, but through this subject is a means of reaching the common man, as we shall call him. I do not mean it in a derogatory way, but average humanity. If you begin to talk about the state of the Earth, the greenhouse effect and ozone layer, then more are approachable by means of this subject. Few were aware of this until the media caught up with it, and brought it into everyday news. Now by this means you can appeal to the average man because he can understand what is going on, and learn how he can help, even replanting trees in his garden if some have been cut down, or suggesting that if there is a local environmental meeting, or if anything can be achieved through voting, then each person can put forward his own ideas to protect the environment from pollution.

You have voted in this way, putting your names upon paper against the pollution that pervades the atmosphere around your town, all from one factory that has somehow got out of hand, and has eluded all the people. Whatever they have done to try to prevent the spread of this pollution seems to be of no avail, but in time their protestations will be conclusive, and will help to prevent any further extension of this plant. Certainly, something must be done and quickly, because it is affecting the health of the public, apart from the general environment surrounding this factory. It is totally out of hand, and against everyone's principles, and most unfair that this should occur when people who have lived in this town for many years never expected any such eyesore to be built. Protest in whatever way you can against any such invasion of your own territory, shall we say, rather like the animals and birds, who protect their territory, you too can do the same for your own town, and the health of all the citizens.

There are ways in which you can help besides voting and protesting against such blots on the landscape, you can make your own garden a place of peace and beauty, and this too helps the environment. Another thing is if you have a larger garden in future times is to try to make a wild section of your garden so that all the butterflies, bees and anything of that nature can feel at home in your garden, and as a result it will be a place of beauty and peace. Truly beautiful because the little people too will visit you. They have promised to I know, and I am sure that you look forward to this in future times.

If you can pass on this knowledge to others who will understand, then much help will be done. There should always be a little area of each garden that can be left to its own devices, shall we say, but I know that it is difficult in one such as this. I know that you, Beryl, had planned to make the top corner a wild section, but it is difficult when it is seen directly from the lounge window, and the lower lawn had to be kept as lawn because you felt it was not worth altering, although you have stayed longer than envisaged in this house. However, in the future you will have a garden that will be as you wish it to be, with little parts of it that will be wild. If you grow trees such as buddleia, that butterflies really enjoy, then that too will be an additional factor in drawing all these visitors to your garden, those trees that have beautiful fronds of flowers in clusters. You can get them in different colours and they will be an asset to your garden.

Q. We wish to ask why cuckoos have the habit of putting their eggs in another bird's nest. It does not seem to fit in with the general symbiotic ways of nature. Interested to hear your comments?

A. It does seem rather against normal ways of nature because they throw out the other eggs or young birds, and put their own in place. I think it is rather like some men who will never change, and who tend to dominate. Most birds in the main are ones who look after their own kind, and do not prevail on others unless they are meat eaters, rather like the eagle and kestrel, who do prevail on other birds, but they do not produce their own young in other nests. There are many birds that prey on other smaller birds, but this is not the case with the cuckoo. They just take over, and quite often the birds that originally built the nest feed the offspring of the cuckoo. Sadly they do not always realise they are feeding someone else's offspring that has usurped their own. There does not appear to be any rational explanation for this. I cannot say that there is anything I can add to what you already know, it just seems to go against nature and its way of life, I am sorry I cannot add to this.

It seems that when you are walking through the woods there is more inspiration than there is while sitting still in your own garden, and there is more inspiration for myself to speak to you. It is more difficult to project my thoughts upon you in a different situation, and more difficult for Beryl to attune to my level of thought. It is an interesting factor but nevertheless a natural one, because I am not in my normal surroundings, and although a Being of Light who only needs to project myself a little further, you are in your ordinary mundane situation, not in the more inspirational surroundings of the forest, and as a result your thoughts are on a mundane level. It is nevertheless the truth, although it may seem rather obvious. I, on the other hand, am trying to instil into Beryl a higher frequency of thought, it is more difficult when surrounded by garden tools and sitting amongst the seats in your garden!

I, Achillion, try to make you think that you are within the woods where you normally hear me. I try to instil into your mind the woodland glade, the larches surrounding you, and the undergrowth within the woodland area that usually has new fruits growing for the season, bilberries, raspberries or brambles, and all these fruits that are so freely given. You see before you one of the little creatures that you feed and he is asking for more. He is happy in his own surroundings, what a busy life these birds lead! It is only when you feed them you realise their constant battle for survival to feed their young ones. It goes on from dawn till dusk as you have discovered. I am now thinking of the other beings who live within my woodland area; those who sometimes speak to you, the little people who you have spoken of today. They very rarely move away from their own environment, and yet sometimes they follow my lead and come with me. Today some of your little friends have come into your garden to see where you live, and they wish to speak also, so I will leave you for a few minutes while they too have a word with you. Farewell for now... Yes we are here, and we are very happy to see where you live. It is completely different from our surroundings and it is so nice to see you. We have not seen you for some time and we hope that you will come and visit our woods very soon, because there are more changes and we always like to see you, so few people know about us or can hear us, and we do miss being able to talk to you.

"Who is it who speaks today?" It is Janus, and I have Olivia with me. She has seen Heather's lovely pink trousers and it is one of her favourite colours also! I know that you do not have long on your tape. Time goes quickly when you are speaking to people who like the same things as you do, and think in the same way. We are glad that you

102

appreciate our beautiful woods, and we know that you take care of everything that surrounds you in your garden. We wish you all well and leave you with our love and blessings. Goodbye.

I will just say a last few words with you before allowing you to have your break for tea; I know Gordon is feeling thirsty! I realise Beryl too has a dry throat; nevertheless, it has been lovely to be able to contact you despite the fact that you could not come to us. I know that you are pleased that I had other visitors with me, and that all of us were able to have a word with you in your own surroundings, and I hope that before very long you will visit us in our surroundings. In the meantime, I give you my blessing this day, and I hope that your work in the future will be of great success, and continue for many years to come.

God bless, Achillion.

COMMUNICATIONS FROM THE DEVIC KINGDOM 3
MELODION-8

We saw your light coming towards us, the light that comes from within, and although at present it is slightly dimmer than usual, normally it gets stronger each time we speak to you. That light of spirituality and awareness, and we know that at present you are still waiting for news, but that news will be forthcoming this week I promise you. One way or another, a decision will be made within the next three days. I know you have waited so long and whatever we say is not truly convincing because until it occurs you will not believe it, but I promise you this, that this time within the next few weeks the business will truly be sold, and you will be free to continue with your work in earnest. In the meantime, we are happy to greet you, and hope you will find peace and tranquillity in our abode this morning.

I, Melodion, have this to say to you, that it is God's will that this work must proceed quickly. Your Northern Light Centre must be established this summer in that place for which you will begin to look as soon as you have rested, and I know that it is something for which you yearn. Everything that has been predicted will proceed in God's time, but His time will be your time now, because you have already waited many months, and you are weary of it, I know. All will be as we have said, and you must realise that sometimes you have to wait for something that is good, something that is essential for the progress of yourselves and others who will come to you. Your group is longing for a security and knowledge that something has been established that will continue for the rest of your lives and for your future heirs to continue. All is well, all is proceeding in the way it should be, and I just wish to confirm this in your minds. Where there is doubt there will be certainty.

I the Bugle Deva am very happy to greet you this day. Think you not that I have been working hard? Have you ever seen such beautiful bugle flowers before? It is through my work and activity throughout the winter that this has come about. I was hoping that you would voice my thoughts on to your tape, because this is the first time I have been able to pass on my thoughts to another, one of the human kind who cares for us, and for the other beings who surround this area, particularly our King Melodion. He is Lord of us all, and we look up to him for our strength. Thank you for listening and I wish you well. I hope the beauty that you see around you will comfort you and uplift you this day, farewell.

We of the woods salute you this day. We have been following you for some time and now have permission to greet you. What a beautiful day for you to come and visit us, it is full of sunshine and the sound of birds. Do you not think that our surroundings are beautiful, if you look at the flowers ahead that greet you, you can ignore the dead undergrowth that is a natural part of woodland. We have been hoping that we could speak to you a little longer today, and this we have been permitted to do.

We hope that we may tell you more things about our life that perhaps you have wished to know and have not asked. We do sleep but not for very long, and then particularly in summertime we visit the whole of the area, all with our own tasks.

As soon as light comes we are up and about and giving of ourselves to all growing things. We receive light from the Source, indirectly perhaps, but nevertheless the light that is given to us to give to nature is from the Source of all. We receive it from Melodion or from one of his helpers, he helps us in this area but his dominion is wide, much bigger than this area. This is our little area in which we live and we are happy to be here. When we have done some work we rest awhile and drink of the nectar of the flowers, and then we proceed once more, checking that all is well. We work with the small devas one of which you spoke to, the Bugle Deva, and together we proceed to put essence into all the living things within this small part of the forest.

Time and again we have wished to pass on information to mankind so that he will understand what is happening on the Earth at this time, and we hope that he will take note that much of nature is being destroyed. In fact, birds are being killed as well due to the atmosphere being polluted, but I think that you are aware of this. When we have completed our tasks we can rest and enjoy the sunshine that is abundant at this time of year, and is unusually so. I think that this has been a month where the sunshine records have been broken, and it is good that this is so because it has given opportunity for fruits to set and be ready for a bumper harvest later in the year.

We know that perhaps you are not certain of your future, but we have been told that you are to begin a new centre of light in the north, and we would love to visit you once you have your own garden, a garden of great tranquillity we believe, and although your present garden is very pleasant, we have seen that, we know that the one you will have in the future will be very beautiful. Until the next time, we will say farewell and we hope that perhaps you may have some questions then, goodbye.

I am king to them but in many respects I am very much smaller than a king in the hierarchy. Nevertheless, I try to do my part as well as I can, and the area that I overlight is quite widespread, therefore I have many responsibilities. I bring down that light from the Source to all the small devas and little people in the large area I cover, that light which is necessary for the wellbeing of all growing things. In this way I contact the Source of all Light daily, which is what you do in your meditation in a different way. We are aware that you meditate regularly each day, twice a day as often as possible, and this is good because attunement lifts the spirit, and even if you hear nothing, it is good for the soul. You are uplifting the soul, your consciousness, to a higher level of being, and that spirituality within you is what is real, constant and everlasting. There are so many who are unaware of this and live their lives on a purely physical level. It is only through the evolvement of the soul that the different layers of consciousness and enlightenment are discovered, and this is why reincarnation is an important part of life, because it is through returning time after time that the soul evolves.

So, you see how wrong people are in their thoughts, that they think there is no such thing as reincarnation. Many religions ignore this fact, and positively reprove those who say it is so, but this matters not if you know in your heart what is correct, you do not need to argue; you know, and that is the most important factor. In looking into different religions you see there is a thin dividing line between each one, and yet each one of you needs a particular belief, and so long as it reaches up towards the Creator and has a balanced outlook, it matters not which path you take, so long as it leads to God, and God may have many names but each one is the one true God of all, the one we all reach up to for life and strength. All that we Devas do is to serve God in as many ways we can, and part of this service is communion with mankind. If man will listen to us, we can be the go-betweens between God and man, and in this way we serve God in a larger context. We can then pass on our knowledge to mankind so that he can rethink his ways that must be changed, so that the Earth can be balanced and healed from her many injuries.

At present the Earth needs as much help as man can give, and it is for this reason that many groups we know are doing their best to prevent any further pollution and destruction. The Earth and the oceans need great help, and we know that you send out healing light each day, and this in itself is good, and we are most grateful for any help of this kind. More help is required on a practical level, and we hope you will be able to do this. We will be able to help you to pass on knowledge to others and in this way the word will be spread.

Different countries need different help, and sometimes money being given to a charity that is trying to help somewhere distant is the only way that you can help, but this too is something that we know is dear to your hearts. All of you do whatever you can in your own way, and if these things are done in a positive and certain way, then only goodness can come from it.

As you leave our abode, I give you my blessing to each one of you that you may receive your hearts' desire within a very short time. I know that you have all waited long and patiently, but I promise you that it will come to pass before very long. Just have faith and you will find that the faith will be rewarded.

Go in peace, Melodion.

COMMUNICATIONS FROM THE DEVIC KINGDOM 3
ACHILLION-9

I, Achillion, greet you both this day, and am happy to see you back in our surroundings. It seems a long time since we spoke last. Now things are moving your way, and Gordon is on his way out of the business after so long. You have been very patient, and he has learnt that conviction that he did not have before. You have all been learning over this period of time, what it is to have faith, and know that what has been predicted will come to pass. Sometimes our predictions take a little longer than we think in earthly terms, but they do come to pass, and before very long you will be searching for that place which you have been longing to find. You have been serving God over this time in which you have been learning how to communicate, and in the future this communication will become easier.

You have had many setbacks, disappointments, and a very long time to wait for the material part of your lives to wind up, but in the future there will be more time to give towards the spiritual side, and your centre will become filled with a great power of light. Many beings jostle to speak to you, beings that are very high in the Hierarchy, and you are greatly honoured to receive these teachings and communications that have been given over the years, and which will come to full fruition once you have moved.

You now have time to take in your surroundings, and apart from the beginning of the wood that has been cleared, and sadly no longer looks like a wood, this part is the same, filled with growing things, many of which are coming to fruition, and you are happy to see that the bird life is still becoming more apparent. Previously it seemed that the birds did not inhabit the larch trees as they now do, and they sound very happy this day. I know that you have one or two questions that you have been pondering about, regarding the essence that is put into growing things by the small devas and little people, that essence that comes from the Source of all, and now you feel that perhaps it might apply to humans also. Maybe it is something that had not occurred to many, but it is true. You cannot function without energies of some kind being renewed daily, and essence similar to that which is given to the plants and trees, is also given to you for your use, and that comes to you from your guide, directly from him, and he receives it from Higher Beings, but all power comes directly from the Source of all living things, the one true God. He is bountiful, and gives of His power to everything that exists. Everything that lives upon the Earth and within the universe is given life and energy.

Q. I would like to ask a question. At times I have seen something like a pulsation moving forwards and back. I feel it must be a sort of cosmic force that goes on all the time, and I am wondering if this particular one is my guide giving me energies?

A. Is the fluctuation a light of some kind?

Q. All I can see is like an invisible, I suppose it is a kind of light I can see it, but cannot describe it.

A. Like an impulse of some kind radiating towards you?

Q. Yes.

A. Yes, this is something that you can see and others cannot, but it is a force of good, the energy being radiated towards you from your guide, and you are very privileged to be able to see this. There are very few who can, so just know that you are capable of clairvoyance, seeing energies that others do not. Perhaps in time if you do healing work you will be able to develop this ability and be able to see the energy centres of the body, the chakras that some people are able to see. Everyone who is aware, knows of these centres but mainly cannot see them, though you in time may be able to see these, which will be helpful in the future.

Q. Yes, I would love to be able to see them.

A. Perhaps your course later in the year may help your capabilities, and open your awareness even further. I know from your mind that you will be meeting one who has been able to see these centres for a great deal of her life, and she has taught many of the wisdom she has gained from many sources, and perhaps she will be able to guide you in the work you are to do in the future.

Most people who do healing will never see these energy centres, and they can function in the work they do without this ability. They know where the centres exist upon or within and around the body, and therefore if their hands are held in a manner to cover the area, they are perfectly able to send forth balancing to these areas. This makes the body respond in a manner that will restore its own ability to heal itself through the healing light that is sent towards it from the Christ. In this way healing is accomplished without seeing these chakras, but if you are able to see them, then you can pinpoint the areas more accurately.

You are very fortunate today to have this area to yourselves, because during the summer at a weekend it is normally busy, but you have chosen a good time, and I hope in the future when you have finally found that property, that I will be able to visit you wherever you are. "That would be marvellous."

I am capable of this, and if you live at a distance from where my area ends, I can accommodate this by coming into your area with your own Deva, whoever he may be. He will allow me to join him in communicating with you, and I am sure that he too would wish to speak to you at many times, with a variety of teachings. There is so much to tell you and I know that at present you are resting from your labours, but it is nice to be able to communicate on a lower level, a more mundane level. I hope that when that time comes that I may be allowed into your sanctuary to join in the blessing of it when you dedicate it to the work that you will be doing there.

"We would be very pleased to have you join us, and very honoured, thank you."

108

I am very sincere in my wishes for you, for the future, and I know that you are very sincere in your convictions, particularly now after having waited so long. Sometimes it is necessary to wait to make you convinced that you are able to do this work. Originally it was rather sprung on you and you accepted it, but on reflection your realised you were committing yourselves for the rest of your lives, and began to wonder if this was what you really wanted. But as the saying goes, having put your hand to the wheel, you must never look back, and once you have learnt of these inner teachings, you can never turn your back upon them. You must walk along that path of truth and ancient wisdom, which is being given to you.

You will meet many people, and some of them will doubt what you are doing. They will twist your thoughts or attempt to, and try to explain away your theories by means of quoting from the Bible or other instances, but you are convinced of what is the truth, and these new teachings that are being given to you, and to many, are those which are the truth. You must be convinced, and be filled with this confidence that is being given, in order that you may help to convince other of your sincerity. I know that you would not force them to think your way unless they were ready to accept it. You will find many who are sceptical, and those to whom you will not mention the subject again, but there will be others who will come and be happy to learn from you, changing their minds about their way of thinking. They will look forward to this New Age, these new thoughts that are being given to many, and they will help you in your work, and be eager to learn. Those are the ones with whom you will decide to meet regularly, meditate and discuss many subjects.

All of this will come to pass, and I assure you that these people will come to you; you will not need to search for them. Time will tell, and you need not worry that all will happen as I have said. Have faith, you have the patience now, and just keep along that middle way, that path of truth and eventually you will come to that place of peace that is waiting for you.

You have been too busy talking to one another to know that we are waiting in a crowd around you, "hello, we are very sorry," well we will let you off this time, but we are very pleased to see you! We have not seen you for such a long time and are gathered around you, sitting on your shoulders, flying and running in front of you, and walking beside you. Many of us are here, all of your friends that usually speak to you, and many more who are becoming aware that you are able to hear us. We have followed your difficult path much easier than you, but then this is our abode and we can fly, whereas you cannot. This place has been quite busy at times recently, especially when the weather was really hot, as you can see there Is the odd trace of humanity here, but fortunately not too much. We are pleased when people come to enjoy themselves in our area, and we like to see people happy in pleasurable surroundings. It is safe for children to bathe here, but they have to be careful not to get out of their depth in the water. It is a good place for dogs, because they too enjoy swimming in the water when it is hot, but I don't think it attracts you in any way! I think that the water needs to be clearer for you to feel tempted in any way to sample it!

In the future you will find your work will take you into many areas of this country, blessing the places that need this work done, and using the holy water that you possess. There is much work to be done in this respect, and I know that you are ready to do so, particularly when the business is completely finished, and that will be very soon now won't it? Even now, it is on the verge of being sold, and we are very pleased for you that you will be free. Free to do many things, and much work of a serious kind, but also a pleasurable kind, and the work is not constant, so you can still enjoy your life to the full with your family and friends. I know that in time to come, Heather will be taking an active part when you are no longer able to continue with the work, but we know that you are to continue doing this for a long time.

She is young compared with you, and although not extremely young, she has many years ahead for learning, and taking part in the work that you are doing at present. We, the little people wish you well, now and always. We still gather round you and will accompany you through the woods.

Anyone seeing you speaking into the microphone will probably think you are writing a book, and dictating ideas and inspiration from your surroundings, so I don't think anyone will think you are being odd. I think perhaps this is something which many people do who are actually writers of various kinds. They must derive inspiration from beautiful surroundings, and cannot always write it down, so I should imagine that many of them would use an instrument such as this for their work. You wish to know about the essence given to plants from us. In the same way that your guide radiates energy impulses to you, we do the same with the plants, holding out our hands towards the plants and that energy from the Source is radiated directly from us and from the other small devas. I hope that this has answered your question. We will say farewell for now, and we hope to see you again soon.

Well, I think that all the questions you had in your minds have been answered by myself or your friends, the little people, and you have had a busy week, so I will not tire you further, and just say, God Bless, and my best wishes upon you and your work that is taking place now, and will continue as long as you possibly can manage throughout your lives, farewell.

God bless, Achillion.

COMMUNICATIONS FROM THE DEVIC KINGDOM 3
ALDENA-10 – Crarae, Argyll & Bute

Welcome to the Glen. Your light is dim and yet I know that you are aware of those of the Devic Kingdom. I am a deva, and I welcome you this day. Like my friend who spoke to you yesterday, who called himself Tarquin, I greet you in this beautiful glen of trees and shrubs that have been gathered over the many decades to provide a place of beauty and peace, for those who come to search for this within their lives. There are many this day who have come to view the scenic beauty. I am called, ah! Now you try to think of a name that begins with A, that is right, but allow me to say my name, I am he who is called Aldena, that is correct, and you have already seen another of those beautiful rhododendrons called Rex, with great leaves, larger than any you have seen before. It is down in the glen, and you will come across it later, but I wish to speak of many things.

People like yourselves who have been attempting to raise their consciousness have been rare, although there are increasingly more being brought into the world at this time who will find it simpler than you, because they have been brought in at a higher vibration, so their abilities will far exceed your own. Nevertheless, you are doing very well indeed, in the short time you have been in communication with our world, and I am delighted at the progress you are making at the present time. Your speech has become more flowing since you sat and allowed my thoughts to come into your mind. It is always halting to begin with, when you first speak through another's mind, and it is difficult for you because you do not know what I wish to say. It is difficult to allow someone to use your mind and voice, particularly when you feel rather tired. Just allow the flow to continue, and do not try to think of anything other than allowing this to happen, and then all will be well. I will be pleased to speak to you in this garden, throughout the time you spend here.

My thoughts are with the planet at this time, which is at a critical point. It is fighting for survival, and although you see this beauty surrounding you, it is not like this everywhere, as you know. So many forests have been cleared for other purposes, and as a result of this the climate has changed, and everything where the forest has been is altered. As you know, rivers have altered their courses and many things have occurred due to man's destruction, but he is not altogether to blame, because in these poor countries man is fighting for survival for his family, and he knows nothing other than survival from the land. There are many things to be taken into consideration, but in future times, man will find that he and nature can survive together if more people can communicate with us, and we can direct and help the way that man will live in the future.

Yes, you are right in thinking that there are many little people who live here, and who would wish to speak to you, however briefly. I will allow them a little time so that you may communicate with one another, and I will speak to you again later on, farewell for now.

Yes, we are surrounding you, and we just wish to say welcome to our abode. 'Thank you.' There are many of us, and as has been said before, if only you were able to see us, you would know that we are alighting all around you, flying in front, and walking beside you. Just try to picture how it may be, and then you will have an idea of the many crowds surrounding you. We have spoken to very few, that it is so exciting to convey our thoughts to you, and to say how delighted we are that we can voice our words on your little machine. Please give our love to all children, and to all who know that we really exist.

So many think they are merely tales that have been made up by someone, but how could that come to be unless it were true? Fairy tales have been given to man over the centuries. Legends that are the truth, and those who have eyes to see or ears to hear will know this. As J.M. Barrie was able to see and hear, he put into his tales for children what was truth, so that children over the ages might learn and know that what they knew in their hearts was true, that we, the little people will always be here amongst the trees, woodlands and the streams. Wherever there is a need for us, there we are. We just wish to finish by saying that we live on in the hearts of all who know the truth, and that is people like yourselves and the children who believe and know that Fairy Folk do and always will live upon the Earth. We will say goodbye, and allow you to enjoy your walk within our lovely surroundings, farewell. 'Goodbye and thank you for talking to us.'

I am returning to you. Within the rest of your lifetimes there will be many changes. I do not necessarily mean the changes concerning the planet, but your style of life. At present, you have come to a crossroads, and are ready, or almost ready, when you have had a little time of rest, to begin the part of your life in which you will serve God, and help man through a troubled time. Not necessarily all men, but only those who come to you for guidance and concrete help. You cannot help those who do not realise what is occurring, and do not lift their hearts and minds. It is only those who wish to raise their consciousness who you can help, they will be of a mind similar to your own, and who are searching for knowledge. It is the knowledge of that ancient wisdom that has been passed down to those who are aware throughout the ages. This wisdom will always be there, available for those who have the perception and wish to acknowledge it, and learn it so that it becomes their own.

We of the Devic Kingdom have much to give to mankind, and it is hoped that more will turn to us for help, for themselves, their gardens and the planet, because through their gardens we can give much that is good in guiding man how to make the most of the benefits he can receive from us. We can guide him as to the best ways to grow plants, flowers and food, because food will be vital at some time in the future, as will water, and so it will be important with the site of the property you will search for, water that springs from the ground nearby. All this will come, and you will be given guidance we know, so that yours will be a safe haven for

112

yourselves and those of your family who wish to visit, and the many people who will come for meetings, meditations and similar instances.

There is great urgency for restoration of the atmosphere of the planet and a balance of nature. We will do what we can in spreading the word, and you must do what you can too, to others who may not understand how urgent it is. It is always difficult to be the bearer of bad news, as people only like to hear what they wish, and therefore if you suggest that unless they change something will occur as a result, then you are the bearer of bad news. Sometimes it has to be bad to make people respond, in order to restore the Earth and cleanse it; everyone will need to change with greater urgency, and use items that don't affect the environment. Fortunately more suppliers are producing the right type of detergents and cleaning materials that people can use. Large industries must be made to realise they are the ones who are causing more problems than anyone, as if the general public were all to respond by using environmentally friendly products, it would still take a great deal more because of the pollution and damage caused by industry of all kinds. Therefore, it must rapidly be brought to the notice of those who are in charge of these industries so that change will occur.

When you look back on your life, you must realise the difference there is in the pollution since you were children, and realise this has been steadily increasing over the years, and you have perhaps visited various countries, but you have not seen the world, and therefore you cannot really see the whole as we can. Try to register in your minds the amount of damage that has been done over the last fifty years, for instance, and realise that this can no longer be allowed to go on as it is increasing, not decreasing. The damage to the planet has been so powerful, that the planet herself will have to take it into her own hands, and it is hoped that man will have made reparation before this occurs. I do not wish for doom and gloom, I wish to give hope to man for the future, hope for man's inheritance of the Earth. Try to be as God would wish you to be, a friend of the Earth rather than an enemy. As you have said, there are books to refer to that can show you the way, but we too can show the way, and through the Devic Kingdom, who you have come across over the last two years, will guide and help you to do your part in restoring the Earth to its former glory if you possibly can.

We of the Devic Kingdom look to you and others like you for this help, and for a promise for the future. The future can be bright, and we know that you will do whatever you can do in your small way to help the planet, and your own part of it, doing whatever you can, and keeping in touch with us, the Devas. We wish you well, both in your lives and in your work and the future, for yourselves and your families.

I say to you farewell, and may God go with you, Aldena.

COMMUNICATIONS FROM THE DEVIC KINGDOM 3
ALDENA-11

Greetings to you both this day. We saw you approaching, and are pleased to make your acquaintance again; it is Aldena who speaks. I am the Deva from this area surrounding Crarae gardens, when I first spoke to you; I am the Deva of all this area. There are still questions in your mind about the work you are doing. You have begun, but in the future your lives will be more fully involved, and I know that the questions are really that of committing yourselves entirely to the work you are to both do for God, and those with whom you come in contact. It is quite an undertaking I know, and at this time of your crossroads in life you feel that you must have conviction and confidence given to you. You know that you wish to do this work, and I am aware of your conscientious attitude. It is just that some have confidence that oozes out of them, whereas others need this confidence given to them, a booster or shot in the arm.

Now, to resume my talk. I know that confidence will be given to you from within, which is waiting to light you up to shine forth from you to others. Even now you are feeling a little more relaxed and confident in approaching other people. In this way you will find that as the years go by, you learn a little more, either from us or the Masters, you will gain confidence knowing that the truth is coming from within you. That truth comes directly from the Source of all, from God who created everything, seen and unseen. So it will be that you will find that confidence and conviction, it is growing and will bear fruit, never fear.

Your companions in this work also are growing in confidence, and it takes a time for all to meld together and unite as one. You still wait for the last member of your group to join you, and then it will be that all will 'take off', and there will be many who will seek you out, once you have established your centre of light. This is something that is sorely needed where you live. There are centres of light throughout the world, but nothing in the area where you live. There are some light centres in the north of Scotland, and many in the south of Britain and the Midlands, but where you live is a desert, where light is waiting to glow forth and radiate, so that we from the realms above can see that light glowing and growing.

As people around you become illumined, they will realise that they have been missing something in their lives, but it must come from them. You cannot put it there; they will come to you, never fear. You will be intermediaries between the two worlds, the material world in which you live, and those who dwell in the unseen world like us, your guides and those in the Hierarchy above. Your task is a responsible one of passing on knowledge and wisdom to those who cannot hear, but who wish for some word of encouragement and enlightenment, and so it will be through your lives. There will be others, who like yourself will channel our words, and so you will not feel alone in this. Yes, it can be a lonely and responsible task in bringing our words to others, and in doing so it does tend to make you feel rather tense, and this is why you need to have a little break periodically, to recharge your batteries. Therefore, this is the reason you wondered why you were still tense in this way when you were on holiday, and when Gordon had retired, and you felt that by now you should be more relaxed, but this is the reason why. It is through doing this work, in reaching up to this higher level of consciousness that you feel drained and you must watch this.

In time to come, you will find that it will become easier as your vibratory level rises over the years, then it will come as a matter of course. You have had to strive, because all this has occurred within a very short length of time, and as a result, it has been more of an effort, but I know that you wish to serve, and in doing this, you are accepting the challenge that has been given to you. As I say, there will be others who will join you in this work, and then you will not be the sole one who channels our words, and therefore, the responsibility is shared, the effort is less and you can give your energies to other things involved within your centre of light.

You have found several places of peace within this area of Scotland, and now you will search for a place for this centre of light. This is something which is in your hearts, and which you will find in the fullness of time. Strangely enough, although you may not think so, it will occur quite quickly, and then you must be ready to sell your own property at a moment's notice, but I know you are not worried about your house, because you are almost certain it will sell quickly, unlike houses in the past. It is a place that should be generally liked by people wishing to come into the neighbourhood, and so it will be that before the end of this year you will be established, and have begun forming within that sanctuary a unity and peace that others will find, emanating from the core of your house. The sanctuary will grow with light from the hearts of all of you, and in which you will bring through messages from those above who wish to commune and send their knowledge to the Earth, to guide all who search for peace within and enlightenment. You will give this and much more to those who come to your centre, and I wish you well in the work ahead.

God be with you and peace to you and all who work with you, Aldena.

COMMUNICATIONS FROM THE DEVIC KINGDOM 3
STEPHAS-12

I, Stephas, Deva of this kingdom give you my greeting. I am sorry you were unable to find a place of peace to communicate with me, but your meaning was understood, and I know that through opening your window you felt you were uniting with spirit outside and around you. When I spoke to you yesterday, it was a place where the church's stillness and its sanctity made you feel you could be one with all around you. The trees were like a cathedral surrounding you, so I could speak to you and tell you how it is with life, how life is an endless circle, and each life you live is part of the soul's journey. It is hoped that within each life, the soul will learn a little more, experiencing different situations, through this the soul becomes part of everything, particularly when the shell or body of the soul in that incarnation is left behind, and the spirit joins those who will continue the teaching in the spirit world. Then the soul becomes one with them, uniting and experiencing a vastness with all creation, actually feeling at one with the Creator.

If you visualise life as it is, with all things, and beings, try to expand your consciousness so it unites with the universal consciousness, and imagine how it would be if you were without your outer shell, just spirit without the ego, the feeling that you belong to no one in particular apart from God. Try to imagine how it would be if you had no memory of your state of being, and your place of birth. If you try to imagine in this way, then you can get some idea of how it is between lifetimes, the time when you are only soul and without any connections, when you can concentrate on being one with everything. When you think of birds flying free above you, you could imagine your soul flying free and uniting with all other beings, with the sylphs of the air, and attempting to be a co-creator with God, as man is meant to be. I, Stephas, tell you this, humanity must improve in so many ways before this is possible.

As you have seen for yourselves, sadly this island is turning into a material paradise, not how it was too long ago, when the island and others were indeed paradise, the climate being superb most of the year, the soil fertile, the people happy and content with their simple lives. Now materialism has gone rife, building abounds and tourism has overtaken the simple village lifestyle. I see these things and feel sad, for your were unable to find a place of peace in the countryside to commune with me, for there were tarmaced roads everywhere. There is still spirituality within the people here, and they attend their churches, and hold that inner divinity, but there is a striving that was not there before. I see these changes and hope that spirituality will transcend the materialism and keep these people free from what others desire.

You have not wished for anything material, but only what is important to you in the future, the crystals you have seen, and I know they will help you and others in the work you are doing. These have come from the volcanic structure within the island, and they are charged with power. You are aware that crystals have a power of their own, but are uncertain about this; you have read about them in books, but are still unsure of their purpose. Each crystal is a living entity, and if you were to have one of those you looked at, you would be obtaining several of these little entities who would help you in the work you are doing. The power you ask for in healing comes from God, and if you have your crystal beside you, then that crystal concentrates the power and directs it towards the one you are helping. In meditation, the crystals encourage this ability so when you reach to God and others, you will be given clearer thoughts and consciousness.

They have been used from time immemorial to help man find himself, and concentrate that healing light. I, Stephas urge you to get the crystals, for they are pure, directly from this volcanic area, and will be very beneficial. They do try to contact you and I know you have heard from other stones at times. I am happy to contact you as I seldom talk to anyone from a different country, or from this one. I overlight this area, and with your ability to receive communications from those in the realms above can raise your consciousness to unite with me in thought.

I am now glad you have come upon our beautiful mountain where there are trees. You have questions to ask regarding the God you worship, and you assumed it was the Creator of the Universe that you prayed to, and is the same for me, but beyond that within another dimension is the Creator of all universes, an immense Being who you just could not comprehend. Even our own God is an immense Being of brilliance, but this is a still greater being, so that each star system has its own God. The Creator of your galaxy and mine is part of you, as you are part of him, for each one of us has divinity within, and that spark unites with God, and God of the star system unites with the Creator, so it is the macrocosm and microcosm uniting.

Keep in mind that you and all living creatures are one, and we are all part of the cosmic consciousness, and all are reaching upwards. Minerals become vegetable, the vegetable become animal, the animal becomes human, and the human becomes guide, and Masters of the Hierarchy. The Angelic Kingdom is a separate system from humanity, and his spiritual system, and so the Fairy and Devic Kingdoms reach upwards to become Archangels.

The Masters reach down to become one with humanity at times, particularly those who exist in the Himalayan mountains, they are close to that Centre where the Will of God is known, and the Masters can assume material form there. You have been in contact with two of the Masters, so you are most fortunate in having reached up towards their consciousness, and I know you hope to achieve more in the future, and striving to reach ever higher to that vibratory level which is one with the Masters. This is good as it is part of humanity's work, to uplift his consciousness ever upwards, and for you to help also in this task, through healing and meditation.

I am reaching upwards too during my reign here, and strive to maintain and improve my vibratory level. I improve my experience through different situations, and attempt to help those who are assisting me in my work. Those who assist me will before long be one with me, and when they reach my level I may move on to a different area. It all depends on experience, and whether the training has been thorough, because we are all climbing the ladder of experience. Remember that Jesus always taught His disciples to strive to be as He was, and live a life of purity, simplicity and truth, reaching out to all, attempting to spread the Word of God to all who would listen. You are disciples in your own way, and trying to spread the word in this New Age. They are difficult times as there are so many who will not listen. Just play your part where you can, never forcing these words on others when they are not ready to receive them, but helping those who are, and give healing when required.

I hope your light will shine stronger as the days go on, but I will leave you for now, because even though the sun shines, you are very high up the mountain and the air is chilly. It has been good to communicate with you, and I hope I can do so again before you leave.

God bless you both, Stephas.

COMMUNICATIONS FROM THE DEVIC KINGDOM 3
STEPHAS-13

Yes, our communication is safe in bringing down the Christ Light to fill and surround you with its peace, healing and protection. There may be noise around but do not concern yourself with this, just concentrate on my thoughts flowing into your mind, and try to imagine how I am. My colours are brilliant as you might expect of an island in the sunshine, particularly one that has a volcanic origin, and therefore my colours are the colours of fire. From white hot intensity to orange, brilliant red, all the colours of flame. I, Stephas, stand before and around you blazing in intensity of light.

This island is one of a group that has been called many names, The Elysian Fields, The Fortunate Islands, perhaps the Islands of Paradise. Many names have been attributed to this area, and indeed in the past I would say that Fortunate Islands was very suitable because they have been blessed with beauty and warmth of the sun most of the year round. The climate has altered somewhat, and there is great warmth when the sun shines brightly, but when the clouds obscure it, there is coolness that does not normally occur, and is due to climate changes as are happening all over the world.

Changes are to occur to the Earth as you know, and have been occurring already through man's pillaging of the Earth, both mineral and vegetable, particularly trees. The beautiful hardwoods have been cut incessantly and not replanted, for his task is to preserve the Earth and its produce. He should protect and replant, and if this does not occur, then the Earth must retaliate in some form. If man does not watch over his work and be a warden of the Earth and all that lives upon her, then he will be struck down. I know there have been warnings from time to time, and mankind is aware now that there must be change in his outlook towards the vegetable, mineral and animal life, but it is becoming more immediate. Man must heed the warnings or else it will be too late to escape Mother Earth's wrath.

It is important for man to be told of his divinity as many go through life being totally ignorant of needs of humanity and the other kingdoms, and think only of themselves, and must become responsible for all life on Earth. Trees and vegetation must be replanted, as the Earth is the Mother of all, and must be honoured for that.

The native peoples of the Earth treat the Earth with respect, for they live closer to nature and are less civilised, but in this natural simplicity, they treat the Earth as civilised man should, and many could learn from these native people. The Hopi Indian Tribe has been forecasting what is to occur on the Earth, and who better to advise the rest of mankind than people such as them, who have learnt many things from their forefathers about the elements of earth, water, air, and fire. Within the Earth are many treasures, energy points that are key points that may trigger off certain

119

changes, and ceremonies taken place at these key points to charge them with power through knowledge given to them by the Ancients. These powers are given to mankind at certain times of history to those who are responsible, and can affect the whole of humanity in either saving them or yielding them to the Earth's wrath, for it all depends on man's outlook when the time comes.

There are seven solar systems that surround this immense, radiant Central Sun, this is where God resides, and they are within several galaxies next to the Milky Way, in which you and I exist within the solar system of the Earth. Other systems exist in other dimensions; part of their system may be seen by telescope, but the rest may be in the other dimensions. I hope all questions have been answered and you will enjoy the rest of your stay in peace.

May God bless you and keep you in your future endeavours, Stephas.

CHANNELLED COMMUNICATIONS FROM THE DEVIC KINGDOM

Book Four

BERYL CHARNLEY

CHANNELLED COMMUNICATIONS FROM THE DEVIC KINGDOM
Book Four

CONTENTS   Page

Channelled by Beryl Charnley

COMMUNICATIONS FROM THE DEVIC KINGDOM 4
MELODION-1

Welcome back to our abode. We saw you approaching with your light shining from within you, and we saw that you carried your small machine, and really meant to speak to us this time. It seems so long since we communed in this way, but we are happy that it is so, and that we meet once again. There is a feeling of refreshment, renewal within you, a feeling that comes from your heart that says that you are ready to begin the work ahead, and we know that until this occurs, nothing will proceed. Now we feel that you are taking the first step along that path, ready to begin, and with more feeling of assurance and oneness with all beings. This inner knowing is most important in your work, and we have felt that it is something that was a little lacking within you, although you have done much work over the last few years.

It is difficult to know when to begin, because you have many teachings stored, and many more will come, but it has to be the right time for all of you before a new start is made, and before that place of peace comes upon the market. I think it will not be long before this occurs. At present it is winter, and the beginning of a new month. Perhaps at the start of this new decade, you will find that for which you have been searching, and know the peace that comes from within. We know that you have all waited for so long, and have been waiting for this peace that does not come easily. As I say, it must come from within you, and for you to feel genuinely that the conviction and readiness is there. You are not expected to lecture to people, in order to spread the word, it is just simply being ready and able to cope with the work, and the pleasant meeting up with people. It is not all work, as you know, but we can see it is coming and won't be long. I, Melodion, have seen many changes happening around me, and sadly, Achillion, whose territory is across the river, and which you frequent more, is sadly disrupted at this time, and you felt you might be more at home here in my woodland area.

Changes far and wide have been occurring, both in the climate and in man's attitudes, and more changes will occur, quite violent ones in the future. You must ready yourselves and others for this, and be able to accept this as part of normal life. In the meantime, we, the Devic Kingdom, hope that you will be an intermediary between ourselves and others, because it is at this time that much help is required to integrate the natural world and man, so that the planet is preserved for the future. Unless more participate in this work, the changes will be almost insurmountable, but we know that you are ready to act as intermediary, and to try to pass on our message to the world of man, so that he will appreciate his oneness with all life, and his responsibility towards the planet Earth.

There is much being done behind the scenes, as you know, in such mundane places as certain supermarkets. It heralds a new day for mankind, when such items as calendars are sent forth to all and sundry with instructions on ways you can help ecology. This is wonderful, and as they were given out and put on people's walls, they should not fail to see some of the help that they can do, both in safeguarding the planet through the items they buy and in recycling empty containers. This is an attitude we hope will spread, and together with your help, and the help of many others of like mind, there will be much immediate help given from man to his surroundings.

The beauty of the Earth and everything that surrounds it, all living creatures and the skies, the seas, the sun, the birdsong, the animals and all growing things, man in one with them, and yet so many take this for granted. They do not always see the beauty surrounding them, the warmth of the sun, the rain, which is necessary for the trees and plants to grow. Everything has to be in balance, and at present there is much that is wrong, the balance of nature is not always as you see it, but if there is too much rain in one place, the floods create havoc. If there is insufficient rain and too much sun, then famine prevails, because there is drought. Therefore, the balance of nature is shown to be very precarious, and if as at present, the Earth is warming slightly, then obviously those areas that at present are frozen, will gradually melt and cause flooding, and great distress if it occurs in a more widespread manner than at present. Therefore, all this must be considered and worked upon very quickly.

There are many who are acting for this end and doing very successful work, which has eliminated much chaos within the world. I am speaking now of those who are helping in their own way to prevent the slaughter of natural habitat, both on the seas and on the land. Greenpeace and Friends of the Earth are two associations who have done much for this. Their bravery is to be commended, and I know that many of you subscribe to one or both of these, and in your own way are helping. It is obviously not feasible for everyone to leave their homes and devote their lives to this work, but for those who cannot, the only way is to help by giving money towards these good causes, and in this way, there can be help given to supply all their needs. In the future there will be more people who will devote their lives to this, young people with strength of character, physical strength, and devotion to the Earth, for the future of mankind. Man must look to the future, thinking of generations to come, for his children, his grandchildren and future generations who will need protection, and whom you would wish to live in a world that is peaceful, unpolluted, and pure, so that they can live in security, and know that all will be well, their surroundings are safe and beautiful. If you wish it to be so, visualise it, and do help towards this effort whenever you can.

We have been fortunate in this part of the country to miss the havoc of the gales that have swept across as far as Europe, and have done great damage in the south and west of this country. I think that in future times, this part of the north will be a safe area, and the south and west unexpectedly not so; although it was thought that the east would be unsafe. They will be areas to be avoided in future times. I am not saying that everything will be swept away, do not misunderstand me, but it is pleasant to know that gales and the worst of the weather will miss certain areas, and this is one that is destined to be quite safe, so you may feel you can settle here without any worries of this nature. There is much to look forward to in the work that you are doing, and everything is worthwhile that you have in mind. Thinking of suffering humanity, healing will be a part of your work, and as we have said before, meditation is most important each day, but you already know this. It is only that as has been said before, through repetition, importance underlines certain factors.

This is a day of beauty, in the midst of winter, and you have had very little snow and frost, and it may be that you will be fortunate as you were last year. I hope that before very long that property for which you seek will appear, and then you will feel that you are taking that stride towards the work you have promised to undertake, and I think now you are almost ready to begin. When you were first asked to undertake these teachings, I am sure you had never thought what it would lead to. To the many beings at different levels who have spoken to you, and passed their words on to others through you, to the pleasure that you feel in communicating with us in beautiful, natural surroundings, almost always in woodland or beside streams. The little people always have this as their natural habitat, and you feel a bonding with them in these places, and with ourselves, the Devas.

You now see the buds that show the promise of springtime upon these beautiful old beech trees, gnarled as they are, and weathered through time. Yet that new growth has been lying latent within them, bursting forth even now at the beginning of February, and so it shows that life goes on through all living things. In plants and trees, their lifeblood is the sap that runs in their veins, as the blood does in the veins and arteries of man, and so you see that the unity between one and another is the same, but different. All spring from the Earth, and all return to the Earth in time. Likewise, the animals and birds, every living being springs from the Mother Earth, and returns to her when their time is over.

Your time, your spiritual time is just beginning, and that spirituality that has been awakened in you, must continue, and spread to others who will receive the word from you, and it will dawn on them, those who are unaware at present, and so it is that time is changing. The time of man's mind awakening within this year that is just beginning, many will awaken to this new knowledge, and I know that you and your group will help all those who come to you. Go forth in strength, in the knowledge that we are with you in this, and hope to serve you as you will serve us.

God bless you all, Melodion.

COMMUNICATIONS FROM THE DEVIC KINGDOM 4
RAMOS-2

Time out of mind, I have attempted to communicate with many who I thought would be suitable to hear my thoughts, and so many times I have been disappointed, but now you have come, the answer to my prayer, and I welcome you both with open arms! You have come for peace on this island, and this is the first time you have felt any peace surrounding you. Your abode is one which is filled with people and noise, and sadly this seems to be the norm as far as accommodation is concerned, for those from other countries, but I hope that this will not be the only time we can merge our minds together as one. My name is of no consequence to myself, but I know that it is important to you, it is Ramos, and I spoke to you momentarily upon the coach on the way here. When Helares spoke to you on the other island, there were many places of peace where you were uninterrupted by those who pass, but do not concern yourself, it is something that we must do in order to maintain the communication between us. It is so seldom that I am able to reach within the mind of another who is living on the physical plane, and I feel that it is most important for me to be able to do this as part of the work in which you are involved.

Time and again you have communed with many beings, many beings of light who wish to make their thoughts known to you. I hope that during your stay, that my companion Helares will be able to once more speak with you. He is from a different domain from myself, and yet he is aware of your presence, because before you came, you thought that perhaps it might be possible for some form of communication between the Deva of this area, and Helares in the south. So it was made known to him, and the one with whom he had communed was approaching this area. I, Ramos, have rarely been able to reach down into the physical mind level, but those people who are able to reach upwards, like yourself, are capable of removing the veil of separation between the two worlds, so that there is nothing between us that need discourage the communication. When you are at home in your own surroundings, it is much easier because you know places where you will not be interrupted. Sometimes the noise of ship's engines affects you, but try to put it out of your mind, and allow my thoughts to merge into your mind. At times like this, you wish that others were far away, those who pass you and call to one another from time to time, but at present we have been left alone.

I wish to tell you that the work you are doing is mot important, and is that of piercing the veil, so that we can speak with you. This work that you will continue for many years to come is being done constantly throughout the world, and increasingly more people are aware of their capability in this respect. The Earth needs much help, and fortunately for the Earth, projects are afoot throughout all the known civilised countries, to sustain and rebalance the planet. Man must accept his responsibility. You

126

know that the Earth has become ravaged and polluted through man's thoughtlessness and ignorance, because much of this has been caused through ignorance, that the seas and land would be impoverished through man's living on the Earth, and his activities whether on the sea or land. What he has done is to change the balance of the oceans, and in changing this balance, this very delicate balance, he has brought about a change so that many sea creatures have been affected, impoverished through something that man has thoughtlessly incurred. Sometimes ships have to wash out the oil that has become used, and in so doing, the sea around that ship is affected in many ways. You commented on the smell of oil and diesel, the fuel that man uses constantly.

I know that you are all aware of what man is doing to the Earth, and so I will not go into great detail, only to say that the Devic Kingdom is most concerned, and I know also that throughout the whole of the Earth, the Devas of all countries are attempting to contact mankind to carry on a communication, so that the Devic Kingdom can help man in his attempts to rebalance the Earth. There must be much put back into the Earth that has been removed. The soil, the Mineral Kingdom and the Plant Kingdom are all at risk besides the sea, and if this word can be spread to others, then much can be done, and you will not appear strange. I know it is this factor that you are nervous about, to appear different from others, but fortunately this is a talking point now, throughout the globe, a talking point that concerns all who live on the Earth.

Each kingdom must be protected, and mankind must unite, the one kingdom of the globe that is responsible for all the other kingdoms, for the future of the planet. He is the one sentient creature who has learnt all there is to learn, and so far through his learning, he has exploited the very planet on which he survives, so unless he can redress the balance, there will be radical changes. I say this sadly; because we must do all we can to prevent any cataclysm that may prevail on the planet, cataclysms that would be irrevocable in their outcome.

I think that mankind will turn the corner and make this a place of beauty once more, one in which all the kingdoms can co-exist safely together. One in which there is hope for the future, and the future lives of the grandchildren of all who live upon the planet, now and for generations to come. I am certain that mankind can link with God, and do what he is meant to do, and this is to serve God and bring about a change of thought, an upliftment of thought throughout the whole world. My feeling is that there will come about a unity of minds. If there is danger threatening the planet and all living upon it, danger always brings about a unity, rather like it did when the war united many, who had never known one another previously, and they banded together for a common cause. This will generate an even greater unity of minds within humanity, because the danger is regarding the future of man on this planet, the future of the planet itself. There are places of great beauty and peace, and these and all other places where mankind abides, must be protected at all costs.

127

This has been a place of beauty, and still can be if man will try to withhold his greed, it is greed, as you know, that is at the root of much of the change surrounding you.

As you saw on your last holiday, greed has changed the surroundings of that island also, but in time, there will be a surfeit of holiday accommodation, and as you have noticed, gradually times are changing, and climate is changing throughout the globe, so that before long it will not be necessary to search out these places, and you will find there will be a general upturn in your own climate. It will be warmer and more pleasant to live in. The winters have already changed, and extremes are lessening. Sadly, there are still places on the Earth where there is extreme drought and famine, but this has always been the case in those areas, and there is little that can be done, apart from attempting to help the governments of these countries that you call the Third World. They make sure that they have plenty, but they care little for whom they are supposed to care for. This is very sad, and we of the Devic Kingdom cannot understand the attitude of many of these leaders, who seem to only have themselves at heart, and not their people.

However, I do not wish to criticise further, only to say that I am happy to be able to speak to you in this way, and to help you realise that what you do now and in the future is vital, to apprehend others of the way in which the world is changing, and has been changing without man's awareness, for the last decade. It is through over-population in many cases, and through the thoughtless use of chemicals, so man will have to try to lead a more simple life, so that less harm comes to the natural surroundings. Around you, you see the beauty of the ocean, with the sun shining across it, as though it had been like this since the world began, and so it has in many respects. It is just when you turn your head, you become aware of others around you, and man's hand upon the Earth where he has changed it in certain ways. I hope that in the future, there will be many more who will be able to uplift their consciousness, so that we can commune with man more easily, and help him to understand what he has been doing to the Earth.

In many ways, the future looks good for mankind, if he is at last learning what has been done in the past to despoil the land and oceans. If he can restore this natural balance, then the future looks bright. My thoughts on this subject are favourable. I am sure that in future times, man will see the error of his ways, and it is hoped that man will realise that what he has taken for granted over the last few decades, will not necessarily continue. Many of the consumer goods that he uses without thinking, may come to an end, but he can live in a simple way, like the people around you. They are happy, and have few wants, so long as their children are fed, and they are comfortable, and have a roof over their heads, they are content without any material needs.

I will leave you now, and allow you to return to your room. I hope that you will be happy upon this island, and that we can communicate

again before you go, for I think other opportunities will arise. Farewell, my friends, and my blessings be upon you.
Ramos.

COMMUNICATIONS FROM THE DEVIC KINGDOM 4
HELARES-3

This is Helares who speaks to you this day. I am happy to be present, to submit my thoughts to your mind. It is long since we blended our minds together in communication, and I have travelled from the south to be with you this day. I know that you are pleased and honoured, I have this from your mind, and I am delighted to welcome you back to our country, to this place of beauty and peace. You have managed to find a more tranquil place today, and I do not think that we will be disturbed. Many things have happened since last we spoke, and I know that when you were on the island of Lopud, and it gave you a tranquil moment in time in which to unwind and free yourselves from tensions and troubles that had assailed you. Now you are ready to start your work in earnest, your work in service to God, and man, and that work that you had just begun when I spoke to you. There will be a place for you when you are ready, and when that place is found, I know that you will be conscientious in the work that you will carry out, and which will be with you the rest of your lives.

In the future, young people will find this work simpler than you do, and although you have worked in this way in past lives, it is only recently you have discovered this capability which was latent within you, and as it has occurred later in life, it is a little harder to maintain that capability when you are tired, tense or things are pressing on you. You have needed a slight rest from your labours, shall I say, but those who are younger and have this capability from the start of their lives, take it in their stride, and will become increasingly powerful in establishing a rapport between the two worlds.

You have done well in the short time you have been working in this way, and I know in future times you will improve. Your place of peace will serve you well, because then you will be undisturbed, and you will be able to uplift your consciousness better, as time goes by, and you will find that you can meditate more deeply in this place of peace. You will have a confidence that at present is missing, and the meditations will become longer and simpler. As you see, when you visit a monastery, most of the monks are missing because they are in their place of peace, establishing their rapport with God. The rapport that you have with me is nebulous today, because you have been interrupted several times. Although this is a quiet, peaceful spot, unfortunately others regard it as their domain also, and it is difficult to find a place of peace in a strange land. I know that you were looking forward to our communication, and I hope that we will not be interrupted any more.

Think of me as a being of light, coloured with those blue, green, turquoise and silver tones, it is difficult for you to imagine a large being of light. We Devas are called the Shining Ones, and indeed we are shining beings of light and love, we are indeed Angelic creatures who serve God, and serve the land over which we have our domain, and I have travelled to join Ramos in his domain, so that I may communicate with you this day. It is now a day of warmth, and I think that you will have this warmth for some time. You have had a short while with rain and coolness, but it is good to have a change in the weather. You are not used to great heat for any length of time, and for you it marks a break within your holiday, that you might establish a new routine with your friends. As you have discovered, you can spend too long with others, and you have no peace, particularly when they have no peace within themselves. It is difficult to change the ways of those who have not seen the light. When you have discovered that inner light, you understand much that has been hidden from you in the past, but when you try to establish this light within others, it is impossible with certain ones, who cannot understand, who have established their own routine within their lifetime, and have no intention of changing.

It is good to try and help them, and to attempt to enlighten them in some small way, but if they cannot establish that rapport, which is the still centre within each one of you, they will not or do not wish to change. They cannot understand and are not ready to understand. Though it is good to try to help them to hear this still small voice, and to learn to listen as you have done. With some it takes another lifetime before they are ready for this enlightenment, but you will have tried, and even if you fail, it is better than never having tried at all. Within each one of you that still centre is there waiting to be tapped, and I know that you will attempt to do this work throughout your lives. It is important work, and I know that it is your conscious wish, and it was your sacred duty to establish before you incarnated in this lifetime, and so it will be that many will communicate with you, to help you in this work now and in the future.

The task of the Devic Kingdom is clear, it is to serve God, and to link mankind with God, to help mankind to do the work he has chosen to do, and to help him understand this task. To help to enlighten all men who have that readiness to be enlightened, so it is that you with your light within you, shining forth, attract many from the world of light towards you, to help you so that it is living proof that your work is with the Devic Kingdom, and all those with whom you have been in communication, including Masters of the Light, lives upon it. Mankind of his very nature has a frailty, and his life is ephemeral, and yet from one lifetime to another, man is learning through experience. It is the experience of living in a physical entity, meeting up with others who affect and transform him in certain ways. Some uplifting, and others who drain him downwards, but never allow yourselves to be dragged down. Always try to uplift those with whom you come in contact that is most important in your service for man and God.

Your work is to link, to be the intermediary between the physical plane and the planes, the realms of light. Therefore, you are in a position to help those upon the physical plane with your communications from the realms of light, to try to make sense of it to others in a more practical way, not in a condescending way. I know that you do not have this in you; you only wish to help in whatever way you can.

I, Helares, bring you my love and blessing this day, and wish you well now and for the future, which is before you. Bring that light from within you, and shine it forth towards all with whom you come in contact. Try to always think well of others, and try to uplift your very self as high as you possibly can through meditation and prayer. I leave you now with my blessing and love, and I know that you send forth your love towards me, and you think well of that place of peace in which we first met. Try to find that peace always, and I will always remember you, both of you.

Farewell, Helares.

COMMUNICATIONS FROM THE DEVIC KINGDOM 4
RAMOS-4

I am here with you now, Ramos from this island of Hvar. If this does not record, you may remember what I have said and retain it in your minds. It is good to speak to you before you leave our land; I have enjoyed so much the meeting of our minds, so that we become one in thought. You with your physical bodies are able to do what we would love to do, and that is to restore the Earth to its former glory, but perhaps through you and others like you, our wish to recover the balance of the Earth can in truth become real. Whatever you do in your own small way, I know that you do it conscientiously, for the service of man and from the love within your hearts; you wish to serve God in whatever way you can. In attempting to create a better world in which to live, and for the future of mankind, you in your way can help to change the minds of others who may not have thought before they spray or kill something.

All that lives and exists was made by God; each one has a right to live. Perhaps it is done in ignorance, or with fear at the heart, but whatever the compelling force, try to restrain others from destroying life in all its forms, whether insect, bird, beast, or indeed trees. There are so many different kingdoms within the Earth, and of course, mankind killing one another, but that does not come into your reality. Those who destroy others live in a different world to your own. You are not keeping the company of those who kill others, but no matter, your thoughts are for the good of the Earth, and I am sure that within the next decade, there will be more who will think in the same vein as yourselves. Try to maintain what you think, and awaken those thoughts in others.

There is much to be done, as you have seen around you. Even on this island of beauty, man has destroyed and changed the face of the island, leaving behind him debris and destruction. It is sad to see, but in the rush for money that man must have to survive, he is despoiling his very surroundings by creating places for others to enjoy, such as the hotel you are still residing in. It is a place for holidays, enjoyment, and some create more noise than others, but each has their own way of pleasure. Some enjoy their holiday in a quiet manner, like you and your friends, others prefer to have a time where noise accompanies them, but nevertheless, it must be remembered that the Earth was created a place of beauty, and man's hand has altered it in many ways.

It has been changing radically, particularly over the last two decades and before, man in his headlong flight for power and money completely eradicates the beauty, things must be changed in the way of humanity's thinking, before it is too late, otherwise the Earth herself will turn on man and crush him, as man would crush ants under his very feet. Remember this, that the Earth as you know is a living entity, which must keep a balance, and man I am sure will see the error of his ways before long. There must be education given to those young ones who follow in the footsteps of those who at present are destroying the trees, forests, seas and land. Education which must be given in a manner, so that they will understand what is happening, because they have not known anything different, and they must understand that the Earth has been changed quite extremely since first it began, and since first man lived in a simpler fashion. You have seen poverty here, and yet there is simple happiness. Those who live in this area may not have much money, but they have beautiful warm weather, and as you have seen, they enjoy it, and almost worship the sun. So, life can be simple and pleasurable, without much material wealth, if man will understand that he must regard the Earth as under his ownership, preserving, restoring and nourishing it, as he would his own family. Remember this, and try to pass in on to all who will listen, and attempt to impress it upon his own family, so that they will spread it to others.

I will not keep you, but I must say that it has been a great pleasure for me to submit my thoughts and feelings about life to you, because you fully understand and appreciate, and agree with everything that I think. I am aware of this, and can understand your concern for the Earth. I give you both my blessings, and every good wish for the future. Blessings on the work you have begun, and will continue, and I know that you will do well in this work, all that you can, you will do, and you will give.

God bless you both, Ramos.

COMMUNICATIONS FROM THE DEVIC KINGDOM 4
ALMERION-5

Welcome to our abode of great beauty. Have you ever seen such beautiful flowers in such abundance? Are we not lucky to be here, and you too at this particular time in the bluebell wood? Always we are happy to greet someone who can hear us, and we welcome you, particularly today, as you felt it was cold, and wondered whether to come. We are grateful, and we look forward to watching your pleasure in walking through our abode here in this dell, leading to the cave. There are myriads of us here, and you cannot imagine the numbers. As you can see by the multitude of flowers, there are thousands of us dwelling here. Sadly, you left the camera but perhaps you will return for it later on, we do hope so!

I welcome you to my realm; I am the Deva of this area. I know that we have communicated several years ago, and I am so pleased that you have returned to this special place. It has within it an air of divinity, peace and spirituality, and particularly so at this time, when all these beautiful bluebells surround us. I am very happy to say that I have been here for very many years, and I have enjoyed my work here tremendously. It is very satisfying to see the result of all the small Devas who work here. See the ferns that grow to prodigious heights, they too are the work of the small Devas, and even though there are trees that have fallen, new ones spring up to take their place. You will see as you go, how much beauty there is in this particular area. This pathway through the tall trees either side of you reminds you somewhat of a cathedral, and this is so. It is like an aisle through the centre, with tall columns either side of you, and the air of tranquillity is like the air within a cathedral, that of worship and peace.

Still the mind and the soul, and this will bring you closer to God. He is watching over you and cares about each one. He only wishes for you to come close to Him and then will be revealed many glories and truths that are within you, if you only know how to reach in to tap them. You are learning, and in time to come, you will become filled with wisdom from Him. What is life for, but a learning place, a school for learning so many things. Experience is part of the learning process, and whatever you experience in whatever way, is all part of life's rich pattern.

Ever since the early days of Christianity, when St Ninian and his followers established the colony here, many devout followers have travelled this path, the pilgrim way in this area, and visited his cave and the Isle of Whithorn where his chapel stands now. It is a route that many have taken in the past, and will continue to do so in future days. There are signs within the cave, of people who genuinely feel that this is a place of great spirituality, and have put crosses here to leave in their names. This is good, as it shows that people still care about sacred things. I know that many live now, who bring the name of mankind into disrepute, but always there will be those sorts, otherwise Satan would not have achieved anything either, but God is happy to see that man is still genuine in his belief in God and in the life to come. You, and others like you, wish to come on this short pilgrimage, to show how much you care, and having started, you wish to complete the journey. I give you my blessing this day. May God go with you, and your endeavours.

"I am the voice of the stream through the trees,
I am the voice of the morning breeze,
I am the voice within the ocean deep,
I am the voice of God."

Almerion.

COMMUNICATIONS FROM THE DEVIC KINGDOM 4
CYPRUS - TROODOS MOUNTAINS-6

We welcome you to this place of wild beauty. It is remote, and yet accessible, and you have found a true place where beings such as ourselves exist, and take care of the surrounding countryside. We are happy that you are enjoying our country, and you feel now at one with it, as we are, beings of light and energy, beings that have existed almost since the world began. We have seen civilisations come and go, and truly we have been here longer than any being that you have had communication with. In this mountain area, it is difficult to find a safe place in which to walk, because there are many snakes that may be dangerous to you, and we do not wish you to be bitten by anything in this beautiful country of ours. You are not used to places of great heat, such as this, and although this is sheltered and pleasant, with a cool breeze, you have been visiting areas that are extremely hot, and which you find sap your energy. This is understandable, because you are unused to this. You cannot tolerate such heat, because you are from another hemisphere.

We live in this mountainous region; we do not give you a name, because we are all one. We do not feel individualised at all, and so it is difficult for you to realise how this can be, but when you return to the spirit realms, you will accept that this is so, and that you will join with the Universal Mind, or the Cosmic Consciousness. It is all one and the same, and so it is with us. We are great beings of light, and we are unimaginably larger than any being that you have contacted. Our size is immaterial to us, nevertheless, it may interest you. We are about five times as large as any of the Devas who have been in contact with you, and I think that they have told you their height is roughly anything from ten to twenty metres high. So you can imagine that we are extremely large, and extremely powerful. Just the same, we wish you well, and are delighted that you wish to be in communication with us. It is rather difficult for us to do this, because we have very seldom been in contact with such as yourselves. Nevertheless, we can manage to pass on our thoughts and our good wishes to you.

Our thoughts are linked with the one true God, whom we serve as do any other Devas who exist, and we have served Him, That, which has always been and ever shall be. Perhaps you think of Him as the I AM presence within you, this is something that He can be, but He has existed over the millennia into infinity. He is That which has always been, which has been before anything else existed, any planet or star. The cosmos came here after that one true Being of Light, who created everything that is and ever shall be. We are here because of His creation, and we exist only to please Him, we serve Him always, and we have great territories in this area. It is a very old part of the Earth, and was under the sea floor when the Earth first came into being. Before we materialised, the Earth was molten hot, and when the Earth cooled, then the various beings took their place, and we were some of the original ones, Devas of this place, Cyprus. What is now in existence is divided, but in time to come, there will be changes, and those who have invaded will be sent off in disgrace. We look forward to this time, but meantime, we wish you well, and we give you God's blessing this day. God bless...

Yes, we are here once more, raise your thoughts and be one with us. We are beings who belong to the hills, the high mountains and the forests of this area. Try to imagine how it is, being a part of this remote wild area. You, who are a part of normal human life, cannot imagine our existence here, and we have been here since this planet evolved. Life is strange, and human life is stranger still. You are involved with others most of your time, and cannot imagine how it could be to be so remote from civilisation, and yet part of the cosmos. Just imagine how it was when the world began, when it cooled, and when civilisation started. We were here before any of humanity arrived upon the Earth. We were a part of creation, we emerged from the sea, and like others of our kind, and we clung to this area and dominated it with our very being.

We have all been here from the start of creation. Try to imagine how it may have been before humanity arrived on the planet. We were here before the Christ, we were here before all religious leaders began their work, and so it was, that we served that God Almighty, That which is, and always will be. All religions lead to God, and although each religion has a different name, it is the one true God, and it is that Great God of the Cosmos who is the one whom we serve, God of all. You wish to be of service to Him, and I am sure that you will be, and are being, trying to serve Him in whatever way you can, and I know that He will be grateful to you for whatever you do. God Bless and keep you in your life, and in your service to Him and to humanity. God Bless,

SECOND DEVAS AT PAPHOS

We greet you, and wish you well. Many there are who wish to avail themselves of your capabilities; I know it has been difficult for you to align yourselves to our thoughts. There are few places where you can attune quietly to our very being, but we have been aware that you wish to hear our inspiration. What is necessary is a clear mind, and time and quietude in which to listen to our thoughts, and to be one with us. You are a child of the Universe, a child of the Cosmic Consciousness, and as such, you should be aware that many beings of light abound wherever you go, and whomsoever you listen and align yourself with. Then it is that part of the Cosmic Consciousness to which you attune, that concerns itself with this island of Cyprus.

You have already had communication with some beings who are very ancient. They are a part of this island, and are central to our thoughts. You have been honoured to hear from them. As they said, they are all one, and do not consider themselves as separate entities, as you

138

do. All who are on the physical plane naturally assume they are separate beings, but once you return to the spiritual realms, then you assume a general universal consciousness. This is a natural part of your destiny, and in time, when changes occur on the Earth, you will find that attitudes will alter, and people will need help to assume their rightful place, and understand what is happening.

You and others of like mind will be essential to the wellbeing of others, and you will help them in due course. The timing of the changes is indeterminable due to man's consciousness, and changes will be less radical if man changes for the better.

Try to help others to understand what is likely to happen, although it is a difficult subject to broach. The Age of Kali will give way to the Golden Age in time, and many are appreciating the need for change.

Many of those whom you know are almost on the verge of coming to an understanding, but they need assistance, so try to prepare them. In some ways, they just need to learn to close their minds to their own thoughts, and everything that is going on around them, and just learn to raise their consciousness in order to meditate and receive inspiration. Everyone receives different things through meditation. Some just receive peace, some receive healing, some symbols, and some have thoughts given to them, instruction and inspiration, which is what you are now receiving. We hope that gradually, there will a great change in the thought waves of man, and that he will be one with us in time.

We are so happy to communicate with you, even in the midst of traffic, you could keep the link. We have not given you a name, but we don't feel the necessity, and just think of us as part of the island. We also, are quiet ancient, and often link with those great ones you contacted some days ago. The island too is very old, and was part of the ocean floor originally, and connection with the great ones is very rare, so you were fortunate to make the connection.

We give you our blessing, to be passed on to all who are on the spiritual path. God bless and keep you always.

That place of peace was found for our work to progress!

WHAT IS CHANNELLING?

For anyone who has not so far heard of channelling, it normally occurs after the recipient has become accustomed to meditating regularly. He or she is used to listening to that still small voice within; not really a voice but thoughts that are dropped into the mind by their guide, or eventually, a higher being such as an angel, deva or a master.

There is normally a signal such as slight pressure on the top of the head, which is what I experienced as a sign to take notice, and to still any random thoughts and listen within.

The ascended Masters are souls who have incarnated many times and overcome every difficulty experienced by mankind, and triumphed over all adversities that man is heir to. They have become true Masters of everything and only wish to help mankind in whatever way they can. They are members of the White Brotherhood, who exist mainly in spirit form, and gather in an area of the Himalayas and other remote areas around the world.

CPSIA information can be obtained
at www.ICGtesting.com
Printed in the USA
LVOW13s1617190218
567129LV00041B/2179/P

9 781907 042317